The Caterpillar Chronicles

Awakening and Becoming in the Dance of Recovery

Melvina Y. Goodman

DEDICATION

This book is dedicated to me, myself, and I—

to the caterpillar who crawled,

the cocooned soul who waited,

and the butterfly who dared to spread her wings.

And it is also dedicated to you—

the reader who may be crawling, waiting, or rising.

May you find courage in your stillness,

strength in your struggle,

and hope in your own dance of recovery.

Your awakening, like mine, is a becoming—

and it is beautiful.

ACKNOWLEDGMENTS

To the individuals who graciously read the draft of this book, and to Ruth—my editor, typesetter, book layout and cover designer—thank you. I am eternally grateful that you came alongside me and helped bring this vision into fruition.

Thank you to all my family and friends for walking beside me on this journey to complete this book. To my siblings, Butch (deceased) Kenny, Geraldine, Theodore, Debra, and Ronnie, who continue to support and love me without condition—I am blessed beyond measure. To my aunts, uncles, cousins, nieces, and nephews—you bring joy to my heart, and I am grateful for each of you.

To my Palmetto Street, Vernon Avenue, and Stuyvesant Avenue family—I am so thankful for the rough, rugged, and real experiences we shared, for they shaped me into the woman I am today.

My deepest gratitude goes to my friends in Narcotics Anonymous, who have lifted me up and carried me with love and strength for over 35 years. Thank you for showing me the dance of recovery and for reminding me that recovery from addiction is possible.

To the pastors and church families who guided me with faith and extended opportunities to do ministry, and to the clergy fellowships that embraced me for my authentic self—I thank you. To the many mentors who poured into me—spiritually, educationally, and personally—I am forever grateful that you believed in me and helped me grow.

To the academic community, mentors, colleagues, institutions, and students—who have opened doors of opportunity for teaching, learning, and scholarly engagement. I am deeply thankful for the spaces you have created where curiosity is welcomed, wisdom is shared, and transformation is possible.

To my sistah circle—where would I be without your continued love and support? You know who you are. I may not be able to name each of you, but you have held me up, shared my laughter, and been my safe place through it all.

To my late mother Shirley—from my earliest childhood, you told me that I was smart and ambitious, and that I could do anything I put my mind to. Your words still guide me. To my late father Ted—the first man who loved me unconditionally. I still remember the days when you called me Splinter because I was so thin, and those memories live in my heart. To my late grandmother Alice—thank you for those vintage prayers and for always covering your family, reminding us that your children are blessed. Those prayers are still working today.

To my greatest joy, my daughter Shéree—you are the best thing I have ever done. I love you more than words can express. Thank you for standing with me through it all. To my precious grandchildren Earl III, Melody and Grant and my beloved son-in-love Earl, Jr, you are my heart's delight. To my bonus children Joseph & Priscilla—thank you for allowing me to be a part of your lives.

And if I have forgotten anyone, please know it is not an intentional omission, but simply a matter of memory. I appreciate every single person who has done anything to help me along this journey called life.

Finally, to my late husband DeWayne—thank you for demonstrating what authentic, unconditional love is. You showed me what it means for a man to provide for his wife in every aspect—financially, spiritually, mentally and physically. You are truly missed. Thank you for loving me because of me, not in spite of me.

Have a great life on purpose!

Disclaimer

Inner Zones is a spiritual and practical approach designed to assist individuals in achieving their visions, dreams, and aspirations. The reflections, stories, and practices shared in this book are based on my personal experiences and are intended to inspire, uplift, and support you on your own journey. They are not a substitute for professional medical, psychological, or therapeutic care.

If you are living with a medical or mental health condition, please continue to follow the guidance of your physician, counselor, or other qualified health care professional. Never ignore or delay seeking professional advice because of something you've read in this book.

The content in this book is designed to complement your growth and well-being, not to replace the treatment, recommendations, or support you may already be receiving. The tools and insights offered here are meant to encourage exploration of your own inner strength.

Liability Statement

Neither the author nor Inner Zones assumes any liability or responsibility for any loss, injury, or damage allegedly arising from any information, suggestions, or techniques presented in this book. Readers are solely responsible for how they choose to apply or not apply the material shared.

TABLE OF CONTENTS

COMBAT: The Introduction

You wouldn't believe it—though you might. While finishing this book my mind came under attack: missiles, torpedoes, boomerangs—distractions meant to neutralize my work. The temptation to succumb to the internal noise was alluring because the inner voices are very familiar territory. Yes, I said voices because that damning, destructive force or what I call "chit-chat" employs my best efforts into ammunition aimed at derailing GOD's plans, purposes and will for my life.

This time, instead of surrendering to the shenanigans AGAIN, I decided to declare war on the enemy. The enemy is the inner-me; the part of myself that operates in fear and resistance at times.

As I settled in to honor my commitment to write daily, the chitchat actively waged war against me. The negative chatter assaulted my efforts with words like: 'You can't do it.' Nobody wants to read what you have to say, Ms. Melvina. You never finish what you start anyway, so what will be different now? You've been writing this book since November 27, 2011. Just give up now before you embarrass yourself. You know darn well that you are not invested in commitment because you are inconsistent. For goodness' sake, girl, you loathe the whole idea of being committed to anything for any length of time. You—Melvina, the runner. Always running away from relationships, jobs, and opportunities.

You say you love GOD, yet you have been running from GOD for well over 30 years. Yes, you've earned several degrees and certifications. You're a professor at a community college, and have even pastored a church. But the truth is, you haven't fully surrendered to the GOD you claim to love and trust. Heck, you started Inner Zones in 1995, declaring your desire to help others get their lives back on track. You gave it effort here and there, but it flopped—just like everything else you do. In 2021, you launched Jewelry Jazz by Melvina, proclaiming it would be an empire—but you've been wishy-washy with that, too.

Oh, and do you remember in 2014, when you celebrated 24 years of recovery and declared that you planned to be wealthy? Not only that, you even planned to purchase an orange-and-green aircraft to take you anywhere you wanted to go. Shall I continue with the laundry list of goals you started but didn't get to complete?

My fellow Sojourners, these are some of the negative internal forces that attempt to assassinate my character and sabotage my best intentions to fulfill my visions and dreams—visions and dreams that are authored by GOD and affirmed in Psalm 37:4 (ESV): "Delight yourself in the Lord, and He will give you the desires of your hearts."

The Narcotics Anonymous Basic Text states: "Lost dreams awaken and new possibilities arise (p. 91)." That voice of my inner critic is fierce and vicious. I am learning that whenever the negative chitchat decides to make a cameo appearance, it is imperative to put on—and keep on my spiritual armor: positive affirmations, affirmative prayer, and meditative walking, all of which help neutralize and demolish the negative rhetoric.

At the beginning of 2024, during my prayer and meditation practice, GOD prompted me to engage in intermittent fasting, which I did for several days. Now, I tend to go to extremes at times, but GOD encouraged me to fast moment by moment. There was no need to be rigid about the number of days or the length of the fast. Can I tell you how freeing that was? Approaching my spiritual practice in the moment was incredibly liberating. During that period of intermittent fasting, it became clear that my spirit was being attacked, and it was imperative to put on my spiritual armor.

Ephesians 6:10-11 (NIV) asserts: [10]"Finally, be strong in the Lord and his mighty power. [11]Put on the full armor of God, so that you can take your stand against the devil's schemes."

Let us not forget that it says put on the full armor of GOD. It does not say, put on the armor of Melvina, because my armor is weak. Yes, my own armor has helped me survive out here in these streets, my wilderness experience—laugh out loud—but time and time again I have reverted to old ways of thinking and old ways of being. In essence, Ephesians 6 is an invitation to surrender my bag of tricks to GOD, and learn a new way to fight, because the truth is, I am in spiritual warfare. I have to fight for what's mine—and so do you. The enemy, the disease of addiction, the devil, or whatever you call that negative force, will not go down without a fight. It's time to duke it out.

After reading Ephesians 6, it became clear to me that the scripture encourages us to put on the full armor of GOD— but it never instructs us to take it off. From a recovery standpoint, the armor is regular 12-Step meeting attendance, staying in contact with my sponsor, developing a relationship with GOD, or a Higher Power, joining a home group, and establishing a network of people who genuinely want to help me succeed. When I forget—or intentionally choose not to keep on all of GOD's armor, not some of it, I put myself in harm's way. Failing to put on the full armor of GOD is like going out into a snowstorm without protective gear: no coat, no hat, no scarf, no gloves, and no boots.

During a telephone conversation in early January 2024, one of my very good friends said: "Melvina, you are in a spiritual dressing room and to find out what fits, you have to try on a lot of stuff." I have never heard it put that way before, but I certainly took her words to heart. Her insight catapulted me further on the journey from caterpillar to a butterfly—the emergence of becoming fully Melvina. Hence the title of this book: The Caterpillar Chronicles: Awakening and Becoming in the Dance of Recovery.

It may sound crazy to say, but I'm thankful that the lower power—the one that resides in my mind invited me to a fight. I am thankful because GOD equipped me with the armor and artillery to win. I declare war on the damning internal and external forces that speak to me in familiar voices badgering and shaming me with reminders of my accomplishments, disappointments, and missed opportunities. It is very easy to feel defeated by that damning voice because it speaks truths about my achievements—and yours—as well as the aspirations yet to be fulfilled. In early recovery, I learned that this damning voice is also known as the disease of addiction, which is cunning, baffling and insidious. I was sleeping with the enemy—and maybe you are too. Little by little, unbeknownst to me, the enemy caused self-doubt to loom larger and larger, until now.

YES, gosh darn it; THIS. MEANS. WAR! It is time to armor up, Melvina. It is time to emerge from the caterpillar stage. I had to stop allowing myself to remain in that stage when I knew full well that I was born to soar like a butterfly.

I am a skilled fighter. Being in recovery for over 35 years is a testament to my skill and courage; abstaining from all mood and mind-altering substances requires authenticity, boldness, faith, trust, hope, and most of all, honesty about my life. So yes, I am a warrior and I am a fighter. It is time for me to emerge from the cocoon.

People who know me will tell you that I am a straight shooter. I don't believe in mincing words or meandering around the point. So prepare yourself for my dry humor, my sarcasm, and many sharp twists and turns. As you read along, if reading my life story seems choppy, that is because my life has been a fantastic voyage. The waters have often been choppy and rough and turbulent. My life has been an odyssey of sorts, very nomadic, shaped by my early childhood and the experience of moving from place to place. I cannot speak for the experiences of my parents or my siblings, but from my early childhood through my teenage years, we lived a nomadic life.

In fact, I consider my theology to be nomadic as well. Being a nomad is a learned behavior, but it is a part of my life that I absolutely love.

Throughout my childhood, my nuclear family moved from place to place on a regular basis. By the time I was nine years old, I had attended at least four different public schools. From those early experiences, I made up my mind not to get attached to people, places, or things—in other words, I made a vow to protect myself from getting close to others. That declaration has shaped my approach to life and relationships to this day. Not only was my childhood nomadic, but my relationship with GOD has been nomadic too. Sometimes I've been up close and personal with GOD, and other times somewhat aloof. Thankfully, GOD accepts me for who and what I am.

The reason I consider my theology to be nomadic is that when I was a seminary student at Virginia Union University (VUU), we were given an assignment requiring us to identify our theology. Traditional theologies—such as Bibliology (the study of the Bible), Christology (the study of

Jesus), Theology proper (the study of God), Pneumatology (the study of the Holy Spirit), Cosmology (the study of the universe), Angelology (the study of angels), Demonology (the study of demons), Anthropology (the study of humanity) and Harmatiology (the study of sin)—did not align with my life experiences, worldview or personal relationship with GOD. I struggled to find a theology that made sense for me.

As I pondered the assignment, reflecting on my childhood and my personal journey with GOD, nomadic theology resonated with me. My experience and relationship with GOD have been a stabilizing force, yet I also experience GOD as moving from place to place, beckoning me to follow the path that GOD is laying out for me. Sometimes, I follow my own bliss, but I am always hedged in under GOD's protection.

This book has been in the works for years, though it had a different title at first. Suffice it to say that, for many years, my nomadic ways caused me to start, stop, beginning this project and then putting it aside for this or that thing. My daughter Shéree—whom I am so proud of, often said that I was quite an indecisive woman. That statement was certainly true then, and to some degree, it is still true today. The power to accept myself just as I am is one of the keys to freedom. That freedom propels me to embrace my idiosyncrasies, my quirky personality, my foibles, and my fair-weather attitude. My attitudes and behavior are what I do, but they are not who I am.

Not only was the publishing of this book delayed, but other goals went unmet as well. The truth is, I lost my direction due to some decisions and choices. For over a decade, I wandered in the wilderness of unfit romantic relationships—sometimes I was the unfit one. Boredom contributed to leaving one employment opportunity after another for greener pastures, and I moved four times within ten years. Do you see the nomad doing her thing, because I do? Looking back over the past decade, it was clear that I was repeating old attitudinal and behavioral patterns of a previous existence. Desperation showed up in many areas of my life, particularly because some of the men I got involved with were frogs—which means that I was a "frogette", leaping from one lily pad to another. Through it all, you have to laugh at yourself—and love yourself at the same time.

CONNECTIONS

Let me share a true froggy situation with you. This is one of the hardest things for me to admit, but I am declaring war on myself by telling the truth. During this wilderness experience I referred to above, I violated the trust of one of my sistah friends. I don't know if you've ever broken someone's trust, but it was one of the foulest things I have ever done. I crossed a boundary that caused our friendship to come to a screeching halt.

When we first met in 2013, we became instant friends. We attended 12-Step meetings together, shopped together, and took road trips together. She always did the driving, because I dislike long-distance driving. When I told her what was going on, she immediately asked, "Are you desperate, Melvina?" I was closed-minded and defensive. I could not see that my decisions and behavior were acts of desperation.

My sponsor and support group tried to reason with me, but in true Melvina fashion, I was determined to do what I wanted regardless of how it hurt my friend. That one decision boomeranged and it hurt our mutual friends, who were caught in the middle. One person approached me in a restroom, right after I came out of the stall, before I even had a chance to wash my hands, and asked me, "How could I do that to my friend?" I responded, "What I do is none of your business."

Some friends were neutral because they did not want to take sides. A few years later, while writing Step 8—which reads, "We made a list of all persons we had harmed, and became willing to make amends to them all"—it became evident that it was time for me to take personal responsibility for the damage I had caused to my friends.

In case you don't know, you don't have to intend harm to cause harm to someone else. Thankfully, when I reached out to my sistah friend, she willingly listened. Then it was her turn to share her feelings. She told me that I had violated her trust because we were more like sisters than friends. She expressed her utter disbelief at my behavior and attitude. After our conversation, she forgave me. Not only that, she said "I love you, Melvina," which made me cry. It was a humbling experience, one that I won't soon forget.

That incident is one of the most embarrassing things that I've done in my life, and yet it is also one of the most valuable lessons that I've learned about desperation, self-will and self-deception. Our initial conversation occurred a few years ago, but it has taken time and effort for us to rebuild our friendship. She shall remain nameless in this book, but she knows who she is. So I publicly say to you, I am grateful for your graciousness and authenticity.

Thankfully, I have not been in a froggy situation since October 2019. By GOD's infinite wisdom, grace and mercy, there was a ram in the bush in the person of my husband, whom I had divorced in 2011. After our divorce, we remained friends. In 2015, we attempted to reunite, but due to my inability to accept the reality of his situation, we didn't reunite.

By 2019, he asked me to come back home—for the umpteenth time. Just a few weeks earlier, I was planning to move back to New York, which I did not want to do, but I was done with Richmond. When he opened the door again to the Ark of Safety, this crazy girl accepted his invitation and ran back home. We remarried in April 2020 during the COVID pandemic. Go figure. How GOD works is beyond my wildest imagination.

While I am grateful to be in the Ark of Safety, I realize that marriage is not for the faint of heart—me being the fainthearted one. It would be deceptive to let you think that since April 2020, I have been brimming over with love toward my deceased husband. Yes, I loved and respected him, but sometimes I was emotionally distant, falling back onto my early experiences and the vow I made to protect myself from getting close to people. It's so easy to slip into old habits when I am not attentive to my spiritual condition. One of the reasons we survived my emotional distance is because my husband was cut from a different cloth than I am—he was not as afraid of commitment as I tend to be.

As I share my struggles, I am compelled to share the great things that I am. I am a lover of GOD, a spiritual seeker, an explorer, a sojourner, a nomad. I am brilliant, intelligent, authentic, ambitious, creative, vivacious, a risk-taker, courageous, bodacious, and beautiful. I am a lover of people, a loner, feisty, fierce, and a warrior. I am a daughter, a sister, a mother, a wife, a grandmother, an aunt, a niece, a cousin, a godmother, a friend, a preacher, a professor. I am a person in long-term recovery, a sponsee, and a sponsor. I am a jewelry artisan, a life coach, a career coach, a lover of fashion, a gardener, a life-long learner, and a wordsmith.

Sometimes I behave in unseemly ways: I can be resistant, rebellious, indecisive, judgmental, self-righteous, critical, envious, jealous, self-centered, unwilling, and fearful. I am all of that and more. Sometimes I compare myself to others, which is unfair. But just for today, I unapologetically embrace myself. Yes, I am the bomb dot Melvina.

At times throughout my life span, it became clear that I was treating GOD as an enemy and an adversary. I was still connected to GOD, but I was distant because I refused to fully accept GOD's purpose for my life. What a revelation—and a hard truth to accept and swallow. Excuse me if you're not ready to hear this, but I have to go in hard right now.

To win the war within, to move from a caterpillar to a butterfly, it is imperative to expose the enemy—the inner-me, the inner critic, including its schemes and schisms. This truth was embarrassing, but it must be said. Melvina has been afraid of GOD's goodness. There, I said it aloud.

Over the past 30-plus years, GOD has given me glimpses of who I am destined to become. Yet over the past decade or so, I have allowed fear to run my life. Fear shows up as resistance, procrastination, getting distracted with noble causes, volunteering, service work, helping people through sponsorship, teaching, staying connected with family & friends, mentoring people, and so on.

I tend to engage in shadow boxing with GOD. Shadow boxing occurs when I agree with GOD's will, but avoid direct or consistent engagement with GOD. Another word for my behavior would be rebellion or disobedience—words that I dislike, but for the sake of argument and overly intellectualizing, I'll use them because the enemy of my soul loves to split hairs, thrives on semantics, and side-track me with bull crap.

Beyond a shadow of a doubt, I deserve GOD's goodness, GOD's mercy, and GOD's grace. For some odd reason, I decided that it seemed easier to battle with GOD than to accept GOD's will and goodness. The book *The War of Art* by Steven Pressfield identifies this internal battle as resistance. Another term for it is self-centered fear.

Let me tell you, admitting that I was afraid of GOD's goodness was incredibly difficult, yet it was also liberating. Eventually, I began sharing about my struggle with surrendering to GOD's will. A light came on in those moments of sharing my raw experience. It became clear that refusing to commit to GOD's will meant that Melvina was afraid of GOD's goodness. It sounds so very asinine to say it aloud, but it is the truth.

One thing I know for sure is this: my authentic voice and my home mirror do not lie to me. Store mirrors lie, because when you try on a garment, it looks good until you see it at home. My home mirror sees me every day, so there are no distortions—except when I lie to myself. Self-deception. Jesus said, "You will know the truth and the truth will set you free" – John 8:31-32 (NIV). That scripture reminds me of a very powerful mirror moment I experienced circa 1994—a moment I describe as a candid camera moment.

CANDID CAMERA

The day started like every other day. I arose at 6:00 a.m., pitter-pattering around for a few moments before starting my morning ritual: reading my morning meditations, sometimes doing yoga, and praying—when I wasn't being lazy. I showered, drank a cup of coffee, and selected my outfit for the day.

Before leaving the house, I stood in front of a full-length mirror, checking my appearance from head to toe: clothing, makeup, even my attitude. Satisfied with the reflection in the mirror, I departed for work, meeting and greeting the public.

It wasn't until around 5:00 p.m., many hours later, that I truly saw myself. I accidentally made direct eye contact with my reflection in the bathroom mirror. I'm not sure I had ever really looked into my own eyes. I froze. I didn't know what to make of it—really seeing myself. I looked closer, and it seemed as if I could see inside my own soul.

As I studied the person staring back at me, I saw the disappointments I had carried, dreams and aspirations left unfulfilled, the life shaped by both pain and triumph. I wanted to know this person, but I was afraid. I didn't know what to say, so I cried. I cried for not honoring myself. I cried for trying to live up to the expectations of my family and friends. I cried because the person I saw every day in the mirror was not fully me. Another me—the me trapped in the caterpillar stage—was trying to emerge.

That particular day, the total complexion of my life shifted. I prayed for the courage to unmask the me I had created. Fear whispered that I was weak, that it had been protecting me all my life. I listened briefly—it was a familiar voice—but then, I heard a quiet steady voice within: "GOD has not given you a spirit of fear, but of power and love and a sound mind" – 2 Tim. 1:7 (KJV).

As empowering as that candid camera moment was, over time, the mirror became dull again. Curiosity—and perhaps old habits—led me to lose my way, at least seemingly. I say seemingly because I don't believe that wandering in the wilderness ruins my chance—or your chance of fulfilling GOD's plan for our lives. GOD does not get caught up in my stopping to smell the calla lilies—my favorite flower—along the way, reminding me that even in the journey, there are moments of beauty, reflection, and divine presence.

Whenever I start judging myself for being inconsistent, I have learned to extend grace to myself, just like GOD gives us grace on a moment-to-moment basis. I don't know about you, but I need grace every single day, every single second of the day. Grace is a gift from GOD, and I believe it is a gift we are meant to use toward ourselves and others.

Did you say something? I thought I overheard you say that GOD is the only one who can give grace. That is true. I firmly believe that GOD gifts us with grace and mercy so that we, in turn, can share them with our fellow wounded sojourners. Yes, GOD desires for us to extend spiritual gifts such as grace, mercy, forgiveness, compassion, and empathy.

These spiritual gifts are far more valuable than material wealth, even though attaining financial stability and abundance is important. In 12-step circles, we often say, 'You can't keep it unless you give it away." To me, that means giving back what was so freely given to me, particularly the spiritual gifts I just mentioned.

Let's be honest and truthful, if a friend was being hard on themselves, I would never allow them to clobber themselves with negative chitchat. Instead, I would offer words of kindness and compassion—derivatives of grace. I am learning to extend that same kindness to myself. Over the years, I have cultivated the ability to be my own best friend, and I encourage you to do the same. It's time to give ourselves a break and extend the gift of grace, no matter what.

CHITCHAT

Have you ever experienced excitement about a new venture, only to be discouraged by negative thoughts? If so, you are not alone. Most of us are bombarded with what I call chitchat. Chitchat parades itself as resistance, lack of self-confidence, procrastination, bitterness, resentment, anger, unforgiveness, guilt, shame, blame, and more. At its core, chitchat boils down to FEAR (False Evidence Appearing Real). Fear has the power to usurp and neutralize your faith.

Several years ago, my daughter published a quarterly newsletter titled *Thrive Time*. She asked me to submit an article which I titled Chitchat. Wow—several years have passed, and I am still plagued by negative chitchat. Here is the article I submitted.

I met a bold and courageous woman named Sapphire. She had experienced the vicissitudes of life including dropping out of high school, single parenthood, drug addiction, and divorce, to name a few. In 1993, GOD spoke to Sapphire in a dream, urging her to establish a teaching ministry. Overjoyed, she immediately called her sistah friends to share her newfound glee, and they were equally excited and supportive.

Soon after ending the call, Sapphire was startled by a sound. Since Sapphire was home alone, she listened carefully and investigated. In the corners of her mind, a cunning voice—the chitchat—began berating her, touting reasons why she was not qualified to fulfill GOD's vision. For a time, Sapphire believed the chitchat and resisted GOD's plan, vacillating and procrastinating. In essence, she did not fully thrive.

Here's the caveat: there is nothing you or I can do to squander GOD's plan for our lives. We may delay it, but GOD is truth, and what GOD declares will come to pass. It might take time for us to get on board, but when we do, the floodgates open. Thankfully, Sapphire was surrounded by positive people—a community of believers who encouraged her to pursue GOD's purpose and plan. And so, she did!

Despite the negative chit-chat in her mind, Sapphire went back to school at the age of 39. Over the next nine years Sapphire earned a Bachelor's Degree in Human Services. Her academic journey did not stop there—she went on to earn a Master of Divinity in Theology, a Master of Science in Patient Counseling, and a Master of Science in Rehabilitation

Counseling. Along the way she acquired numerous professional certifications and recently became a licensed professional counselor. Today, she is pursuing a doctoral program studying addiction, religion and spirituality.

Sapphire is a college professor, and served as a program manager at a residential substance abuse treatment facility for ten years. Along life's journey, she learned that it is easy to lose heart and direction. During turbulent times, she discovered the importance of staying connected to her community of believers, who encouraged and motivated her to keep moving forward.

Can you identify with Sapphire? Well, I certainly can, because Sapphire's real name is Melvina. Choosing the name Sapphire was a literary decision to tell my story in the third person. Not only that, Sapphire is my birthstone color. I invite your inner Sapphire to come out of the cocoon and thrive!

There are biblical examples of people who experienced chitchat. Consider the stories of Moses (Exodus 3 & 4), Naomi (Ruth 1), Jonah (Jonah 1-4), Mary (Luke 1:26-38), and Jesus (Matthew 4:1-11 & Luke 22:39-42). Are you clearing your throat in that tone that says Ms. Melvina, you're treading on shaky ground now? Yes, fellow sojourner, I can hear your question, and it is not rhetorical. Your question might go something like: Ms. Melvina, what do you mean that Jesus experienced chitchat? I invite you to read the biblical stories for yourself with an open mind.

During the wilderness experience, Jesus faced numerous obstacles and challenges set up by the enemy as failure tactics—or more accurately, the devil enticed Jesus to be disobedient. Matthew 4 tells the story of the battle between human desires, the enemy's tricks, and GOD's will. In essence, what took place in the wilderness between Jesus and the devil was a battle royal. When GOD gives us a purpose, a negative force will often attempt to lure us into self-aggrandizement. Don't be intimidated by the chitchat. There will be times when your will and your mind are under attack, but keep the faith. The chatter is only a scare tactic designed to keep you stagnant.

Have you ever requested that GOD remove something you didn't want to deal with? The narrative in Luke 22 provides another example of Jesus battling chitchat. Biblical stories often seem as if events occur immediately, but some things unfold over time.

In Luke 22, Jesus asks GOD to remove the cup of suffering from him. In my view, it seems Jesus experienced second thoughts about taking on the sins of the world, even though he knew that was his divine purpose. Remember, Jesus was both human and divine and we, too, possess both aspects—so give yourself some grace.

Jesus demonstrated what it means to commit fully to GOD's purpose, while also wrestling with self-will. He overcame it by affirming, "Not my will, but your will be done." Maintaining commitment to GOD—or anything meaningful— is not easy when our minds are flooded with swirling thoughts. Fear manifests in the realities and challenges of life: financial struggles, abandonment issues, marital or relationship discord, intimate partner violence, addiction, childhood abuse, mental health conditions, loss of dreams, unemployment, homelessness, aging, and health concerns.

Self-doubt can creep in, threatening to contaminate our faith, making it difficult—but NOT impossible to move toward and achieve the things GOD has purposed for us.

GOD's response to our chitchat is a resounding "SO WHAT?!" GOD will entertain our objections and even our folly, but GOD is not moved by our fear. GOD shuts down our chitchat expeditiously. Why? Because GOD is focused on using our story to bring glory to GOD. It is time to come out of the caterpillar stage, Melvina!

Instead of allowing the negative chitchat to win, let's take encouragement from how Jesus handled the situation. At first, Jesus listened to the noise in his head, but eventually, He exhibited courage and boldness by standing firm against the chitchat. And so can we. Let's stand on our faith, no matter what. Don't forget to reach out to your community of believers when your faith is challenged. You've got this. Go on with your bad self!

Spoiler Alert: That was not the last time that fear trapped Melvina off, and chances are it will happen again. Now, the invitation is extended to YOU; yes, YOU. I invite you to sojourn with me on this fantastic voyage called life. I have decided to be intentional about what I want, rather than allowing the chitchat to neutralize my efforts. To thrive, it is imperative to focus on the here and now—maintaining an attitude of gratitude and practicing affirmative prayer, meditation, and mindfulness. Practicing spiritual principles is the fuel we need to transport us toward our destiny, and they are our ammunition against the enemy of our soul.

COMPLAIN

I wholeheartedly believe that we need to allow ourselves to feel sad, meaning we have the right to complain. Although some people will beg to differ, that is fine. Unfortunately, our families and society at large have taught us to suck it up. We are expected to keep moving forward despite being afflicted with a broken heart, being spiritually bereft, suffering from splintered limbs, or being grief-stricken, mentally and emotionally spent—all of which can leave us feeling disoriented, disinterested, discombobulated, and disgusted.

Today, grant yourself permission to bemoan and commiserate over all the things that tried to defeat you and keep you from embracing GOD's purposes and plans for your life. Identifying and acknowledging past hurts and violations is vital to your overall well-being. I have allowed myself to fully feel and wallow in my emotions because it is necessary. My past experiences have provided insight and clarity into the situations and circumstances that once drove me to my knees, my bed or my couch.

Therefore, you are strongly encouraged to wallow in sadness because it provides an opportunity for us to pivot. Give yourself permission to lambast, cuss, and fuss about people and systems that violated your trust. Go ahead—throw yourself a pivot party—because your best self is right there on the horizon, waiting for you to discard the old self. Go ahead now. Don't miss the chance to confront and commiserate over the experiences that have held you hostage and confined your spirit. The truth is, without those very situations and circumstances, we would not have arrived at this place of transformation.

Some of the darkest moments in my life have given me inner strength and fortitude—a weapon we can use to deactivate the inner critic and neutralize the negativity of others.

As we move forward, let's focus on what we want, rather than what we don't want. What has been is just that— it already happened. In other words, "It is what it is and it ain't what it ain't." Moving forward on this quest I choose to be fully present to what is, and what is yet to come.

Typically, I allow myself to mope and complain for 1-3 full days. Maybe there is something spiritual in the number three: the Trinity—Father, Son and Holy Spirit; me, myself and I; the sun, the moon, and the stars. And don't forget, Jesus resurrected after three days.

Come on—let's get back on the playing field of life. Ready, set, GO! Are you ready for the next stage of becoming fully YOU; a beautiful butterfly?

CHRYSALIS STAGE

What comes to mind when I say the word chrysalis? If you envision a cocoon, then you are correct. Think of yourself as a caterpillar in preparation for becoming a butterfly, embodying all that GOD, the Creator, designed you to be.

The emergence of a butterfly has always fascinated me, especially because it begins as a caterpillar—a member of the worm family. As a child, whenever a caterpillar crossed my path, I would step on it. To me, they looked creepy and ugly. From the outside, there was nothing beautiful about a caterpillar. But later, I learned that within every caterpillar, is a butterfly awaiting its time to emerge.

Many years ago, a dear male friend introduced me to a book titled *Hope for the Flowers*, and it forever changed my perspective on caterpillars. It's a book I read from time to time.

I am a lover of butterflies. They are so beautiful that whenever I see one, I pause—everything else takes a backseat. To me butterflies represent transformation. On two separate occasions, I was blessed to see a black butterfly, and both times it took my breath away. Once, while I was on the phone with a friend, a black butterfly landed on a plant leaf and lingered just long enough for me to capture a picture of it. Thank you, God, for allowing the butterfly to show its beauty. Immediately, the song *Black Butterfly* by Deniece Williams came to mind. The lyrics are poetic, powerful and uplifting. If you haven't heard it before, I invite you to take a moment and listen—it will bless your soul.

Within every living thing, lies hidden potential—an invitation to become greater than what the naked eye can see. The same holds true for us. So go ahead, look at yourself in a mirror again. If you peer deeply into your eyes, you will discover something extraordinary: a butterfly, a jewel, a new you emerging even in this very moment.

Ain't GOD exceptional? When you looked, I know you caught a glimpse of GOD's unique handiwork and craftsmanship shining through you.

During the chrysalis stage, you may find yourself filled with fresh ideas about the life you want to create and the things you hope to manifest. This sacred stage is not just about waiting—it's a time of preparation, restoration and refreshment. While you're incubating in your chrysalis, you might be inspired to launch a business, return to school, write a book, or travel to new places.

Don't let those ideas slip away. Write them down. Pray about them. Reflect on them. Conduct research into your interests and curiosities so that when the time comes to spread your wings, you'll have the insight and direction you need to step boldly into the next chapter of your life.

Many people struggle with discerning GOD's will for their lives, so if that's you, know that you are not alone. Often, we overcomplicate the process. If you want to know GOD's will and purposes for your life, simply ask GOD, and GOD will tell you.

One thing I've learned is this: there's a big difference between hearing and listening. Hearing happens naturally; you don't have to make an effort to catch the sounds of the wind blowing, birds singing, rain falling, or the hum of your house when the TV and radio are turned off.

But listening— that's different. I'm working on listening because listening requires leaning in. When I lean in to a conversation, I don't just hear words. I'm engaging with my mind, my heart, my spirit, my eyes, and my ears. I listen to understand first, and only then if I need clarity, do I ask questions. My hope is that I will learn how to listen fully before interrupting.

We can apply those same listening skills when discerning GOD's will and purposes for our lives. All it takes is being quiet, leaning in, and truly listening. Try it and see for yourself.

COMMUNITY OF BELIEVERS (COB)

Earlier in this book, I made reference to the importance of a community of believers. I want to pause here and expand on that thought, because having a dependable faith community is essential on this journey.

To thrive against all odds and fully emerge into the butterfly version of yourself, you will need a community of believers, a tribe that can walk with you on your quest. I don't know about you, but I certainly need accountability, affirmation, encouragement and direction. Don't allow the "chitchat" and the ugliness of your caterpillar stage to kill your butterfly before you even emerge.

Ecclesiastes 4:9-12 (NIV) declares, [9]"Two are better than one, because they have a good return for their labor. [10]If either of them falls, one can help the other up. But pity anyone who falls and has no one to help them up. [11]Also, if two lie down together, they will keep warm. But how can one keep warm alone? [12]Though one may be overpowered, two can defend themselves. A cord of three strands is not quickly broken."

The goals I discussed in this book were made possible because I had a community of believers (COB). In 12-step circles, we call it a support network—a group of people who encourage me to pursue my aspirations. Both women and men believed in me, and my family believed in me, particularly my mother, who always reminded me that I was smart and ambitious. If you don't have a community of believers, I encourage you to establish one, because you will certainly need people to uplift and remind you of who you are when the enemy attempts to assault your intentions. You will also need this community— if and when you start to meander and wander off course.

In 12-step circles, it is suggested that we find at least one person who believes in us and wants to help us in our recovery. Those of us who belong to 12-step fellowships understand the necessity of being surrounded with people on the road to recovery. It is suggested to obtain a sponsor, and to develop a recovery network of people who practice the principles of the program in their daily lives.

In 1990, when I was introduced to Narcotics Anonymous, I was afraid to ask for help because asking for help was a foreign concept to me. I was someone who, at age 17 made a silent pact with myself that 'no one would ever hurt me again'—an inaudible commitment I made after my first romantic relationship went awry. I had been independent most of my life, making my own decisions and relying on myself; I didn't fully trust people to have my best interests at heart. While I didn't have trust issues in friendships, romantic relationships which require intimacy (in-to-me-see), loomed large with distrust. Even friendships require intimacy. For me, to humbly ask another person for help required an act of GOD.

Eventually, I mustered up the courage to ask someone to sponsor me, and that decision has proven to be one of the best decisions I've ever made. Over the past 35 years, different women have sponsored me, and each one of them has been instrumental in my growth and maturation. Each one, in her unique way, guided and encouraged me to practice self-love, honesty, open-mindedness, willingness, and self-acceptance—lessons that helped me discover my authentic self.

As I have grown and evolved, I realize that, for the most part, what I have been striving for is my authentic voice and the ability to be unapologetically me. Beyond any other attribute, authenticity is my greatest asset. I recognize that authenticity does not mean avoiding choices that may yield unfavorable results, like some of the ones I mentioned earlier. I love Melvina regardless of what I have said or done in the past.

In addition to sponsorship, God has graced me with the privilege of having meaningful relationships with my daughter, siblings, relatives, sistah friends, incredible women and men in recovery. I also have been blessed by church congregations who have graciously provided emotional, spiritual, and financial support throughout my journey. GOD placed these people in my path, and for that, I am eternally grateful.

The foundation of my spiritual formation is rooted in Christianity and 12-step recovery. Being a member of a 12-step fellowship gave me the liberty and freedom to investigate other faith traditions, including Yoruba, Santeria, African cosmology, Egyptian Kemetic spirituality, Hinduism, Buddhism, and Kabballah. I also learned about the chakras, reiki, aromatherapy, and so much more.

My understanding and relationship with GOD started as a biblical perspective, but it has since evolved, because GOD is bigger than any religious or spiritual book written about GOD. I would describe my religious/spiritual understanding of GOD as eclectic, though biblical theology is the bedrock of my faith journey. That might sound sacrilegious to some, but it is true for me, and it has served me very well. Please don't take offense; it is not meant to be disrespectful to anyone's belief system. Your relationship with GOD is your own, and it is none of my business.

Two are indeed better than one, as it says in Ecclesiastes 4:9-12. When you feel like giving up and you are tempted to quit, I hope you will recognize and appreciate the extraordinary people in your midst. If you're unsure of who to trust, allow GOD to guide your path. Remember, to bring your vision to fruition, you need people, because it's easy to lose momentum along the way. Always remember that with GOD on your side and with people who believe in you, nothing is impossible for you.

That brings to mind the story of Mary & Elizabeth in Luke 1:39-56. After Mary's conversation with an angel regarding the conception of Jesus, she visited her older cousin Elizabeth. Mary immediately sought support to help her understand GOD's vision. Can you identify with Mary? I can, because it can be challenging to wrap your mind around GOD's seemingly preposterous plan. Granted, GOD probably didn't call you or me to bring forth the Christ, but the vision GOD entrusted to you and me is equally important. Let's be like Mary & Elizabeth by supporting the purposes GOD entrusted to each one of us. As a part of your COB, consider including a life coach as a part of your support system.

Over the past 20 years, I've had the privilege of coaching and assisting many people in fulfilling their visions. A couple of years ago, I became a certified life coach. I've had some paid clients, and I am still building my brand. As I've mentioned, the chitchat has paralyzed me at times because I allowed my faith to atrophy. It takes courage to live your dream, no matter what the internal and external chatter says.

COURAGE

Did you know that courage, faith, and doubt are close relatives? It takes courage to be your authentic self, to actualize your vision, and to trust GOD. Courage is not an absence of fear or doubt. In my mind, courage, faith, fear, and doubt are actually homegirls and homeboys—they all roll together.

When we look at ourselves—our resources, circumstances, pedigree, marital status, and everything else—it is easy to surmise that the challenges ahead are far too great to press forward. Yes, I said challenges, because we will face some formidable opponents on this journey of unfolding into our true selves. It is tempting to ignore the chitchat, but to combat it, you must first know what it is saying and what ammunition it uses to derail you. Often it plays on the things you least expect. Listen to that mere dissenting inner critic, but do not fall prey to its ignorance. Remember, fear, resistance, and comparing ourselves to others provide valuable information, but we cannot allow negative chitchat to paralyze us or trigger self-doubt. In Matthew 17:20 (NIV), Jesus said: "For truly I tell you, if you have faith as small as a mustard seed, you can say to this mountain, 'Move from here to there,' and it will move. Nothing will be impossible for you."

Several years ago, I purchased some mustard seeds because I was curious as to why Jesus equated mustard seeds with faith. I was very surprised at how tiny they were. I decided to plant some to see what would happen. Within three days, the seeds sprouted. WHOA! I could not believe it. After that experience, I began to understand Jesus' mustard seed analogy more deeply. In essence, a small seed of faith can accomplish wonders on our faith journeys. I encourage you to try it yourself—plant some mustard seeds in a flower pot to see what unfolds.

For my 24th recovery anniversary, I packaged and gifted mustard seeds to friends who attended the celebration. Within days, I received many phone calls from people excitedly sharing how the seeds had germinated. Witnessing the miracle strengthened their faith in themselves and in GOD—and it strengthened mine as well. One of my favorite scriptures is Joshua 1:9 (NIV): "Have I not commanded you, only be strong and very courageous. Do not be afraid; do not be discouraged, for the Lord your GOD will be with you wherever you go."

In 2001, when I moved from Brooklyn, NY, to Richmond, VA (RVA) to attend seminary at The Samuel DeWitt Proctor School of Theology at Virginia Union University (VUU), Joshua 1:9 became my personal motto. In my heart of hearts, I knew that VUU was the school where I was meant to be educated. After submitting all of the necessary documents, I eagerly awaited my acceptance letter. My stance at the time was that there was no conceivable reason for my application to be denied, so I began preparing for the move. There was so much to do: resign from my job, terminate my lease, obtain an apartment in RVA, pack my belongings, order a U-Haul, find someone to drive the truck, plan a farewell celebration, and say so long to my daughter, my mother, my family, and my friends.

In July of 2001, I found a beautiful affordable garden apartment. The RVA rental office informed me that I had to move in by Saturday, August 11, 2001—my daughter's birthday— or forfeit the apartment. At that point, I still had not received my acceptance letter from VUU. The administrative assistant told me that my pastor had not sent the required documentation. Can I tell you that I had crazy faith at that time? On Friday, August 10, the day before my scheduled move, I called VUU again, and I got the same answer. My heart plummeted, but I kept the faith despite feeling disappointed. I called my church, and my pastor promised to send the documentation, but he didn't. For some reason, I was not worried. I believed VUU was where I was supposed to be educated. I was packed and ready to go, along with my belongings and my faith—another one of my most prized possessions. The missing letter did not stop me; it propelled me forward. I pressed on toward my goal, trusting in GOD. With my faith in tow, and trust in GOD, we loaded the U-Haul with my belongings, and attached my 1989 Plymouth Sundance, a gift from my cousin years earlier. It was an exciting time.

Seminary was scheduled to start on Tuesday, September 11, 2001—the day the World Trade Center was attacked by terrorists and airplanes. I happened to be watching the news when the airplanes hit the Twin Towers. My first instinct was to check on my loved ones, and thankfully they were safe. I didn't know any friends in RVA at the time, so I stayed home, glued to the television, absorbing the shock and the unfolding horror.

A few days before classes were set to start, I visited VUU to meet with the dean. He informed me that my pastor had sent the recommendation letter a few days earlier. Looking back, I realize that my faith— and my signature cowboy boots were made for walking in faith. LOL!!! Wow, how I miss that girl with her foolish, courageous faith. That entire experience is living proof that faith without works is dead (James 2:14-26, KJV). That was then, and this is now! Hebrews 11:1 (KJV) reads, "NOW (emphasis mine), faith is the substance of things hoped for and the evidence of things not seen."

Shall I repeat that? NOW faith means faith in this moment—right here, right now, not the faith of yesteryear or yesterday, but the faith of the present. I cannot go back to who I used to be, but I can learn from the past, and remember that the faith-filled foolish girl named Melvina still resides within me. I hope you see why courage is required to fulfill your GOD given visions and dreams. The mind—oh the mind is a battlefield. Take courage and fight! Come on, step out of the cocoon.

COMPARE

Let's talk about a culprit that undermines our best efforts, at least it has undermined me. That culprit is a negative force called comparison. Perhaps you've been comparing yourself to others. Whenever I compare myself, I always come up short, no doubt about it. From the outset, be reminded: you and I are unique. There is no one else in this world like you or like me. Begin to appreciate yourself fully, including your idiosyncrasies, your foul ups, your bleeps, your blunders, your skills, your talents, and your abilities.

There have been times in my life when I compared myself to others. In the 1980's during the powder cocaine season of my life, it was difficult to see that my drug use had gotten out of control. I loved snorting powder cocaine, often lacing my Newport cigarettes to intensify the euphoric experience. I also typically drank a pink champale or a tequila sunrise. One reason I didn't recognize my drug problem was due to comparing myself to my sister's best friend, who was addicted to crack cocaine. Her rapid decline was easy to see, but I couldn't see my downward spiral, because in my mind she looked bad. She was intelligent; had a good paying job in

Manhattan, and she was a sharp dresser. Unfortunately, she got caught up in free-basing and smoking crack, which contributed to her demise. Unfortunately, she died, whether from her drug use or not, I don't know. I'm using her as an example because comparisons don't help us to see ourselves—they only delay the inevitable, and blind us to our own realities.

In case you don't know, there is such a thing as a functional drug or alcohol user. Many people, myself included, use or used drugs while still maintaining employment, housing, and caring for their children. Be that as it may, my dependency on drugs ultimately caused my life to go nowhere fast.

Let me give you another example of how comparing ourselves to others can keep us stuck. It is easy to look at someone who is highly successful—a person in long-term recovery, a televangelist, a talk show host, a preacher, or a celebrity—and think, I could never achieve that level of success. It's also easy to compare ourselves to someone who seems worse off and say, *At least I'm not that bad.* On the flip side, comparing ourselves to highly successful people and believing we'll measure up can also trap us. Engaging in this type of self-talk eventually can lead to a mediocre existence. Making excuses, gives us permission to remain in the cocoon—a place that initially serves as a stage of preparation, but when fear takes hold, it can become a place of mediocrity, stagnancy & complacency.

In Numbers 13, the Israelites were sent to explore Canaan, the land that God had promised them. Upon arrival, they saw giants and viewed themselves as mere grasshoppers. Fear overtook their faith—their legs buckled, their faith wavered, and they trembled inside and out—even though GOD had already assured them of victory long before they pursued the land. Isn't it remarkable how GOD repeatedly assures us of GOD's omnipresence (always there), omnipotence (all-powerful), and omniscience (all-seeing), yet we still doubt GOD. Like the Israelites, we are called to trust and believe GOD, no matter what we see or feel.

Comparing myself to real or imagined giants and grasshoppers heightened my feelings of inadequacy, insecurity, and insufficiency. As a result, I often excluded myself from the clergy world in particular, keeping myself trapped in a self-imposed prison. Living Clean: The Journey Continues puts it well: "Our self-made prisons no longer serve us. We are free to explore and discover what we are good at. We are free to participate, create, care, and share, surprise ourselves, take risks, be vulnerable, and stand on our own two feet. We find our beliefs and begin to act on them. We make decisions based on our values. We walk through fear and wake up to the miracles that surround us, we are free to be who we are and live as we choose" (p.5).

I refuse to succumb to the war tactics of the inner critic, which berates me with negative nonsense. Melvina is a risk-taker. Melvina knows how to walk through fear. Melvina knows how to walk in faith. So walk on, girl! The chorus to the 1966 song by Nancy Sinatra 'These Boots Are Made for Walking' says it better than I can:

"These boots are made for walkin', and that's just what they'll do, one of these days these boots are gonna walk all over you."

Not one day—these boots aren't waiting for the future. Today, this very day, these boots are walking all over the enemy, over the inner me.

Well, TODAY is the day. Today, these boots are walking all over the enemy. I declare and decree that I will keep my dukes up and my spiritual armor on, because it is time for me to step into the arena where GOD wants me to be. Am I fearful to take the next step? Absolutely. But I am tired of running from GOD's goodness. So I ask you: Whose report shall you believe—the perceived giants: Say it with me: I believe GOD no matter what. Say it aloud three times: I believe GOD no matter what. I believe GOD no matter what. I believe GOD no matter what.

49

CALLING (Voice)

News Flash: GOD entertained my folly for years. I learned that GOD allowed me to think that I was winning when, in fact, I was losing. Read Jacob's story in Genesis 32:22-32. The gist of the story is that Jacob wrestled with an angel—or a man, or maybe even a woman. After all, he was a womanizer. Or maybe it was GOD he wrestled with. In the end, Jacob won, but he walked away with a limp. Yeah, I too have been resisting and wrestling with GOD. But enough is enough. I will never win going up against GOD, so I may as well surrender... or end up limping, Shaking my head. So I choose to surrender.

A calling is a mysterious thing, at least to some of us. When we hear the word 'calling', we might even begin to tremble. In my view, calling and purpose are synonymous, yet discerning one's calling is often challenging. In 1993, I received a clear message from GOD that I was called to preach. OH NO!!! With expediency, I went into rejection/resistance mode. In my mind, there was no way that GOD could use me. But those thoughts were rooted in my limited view of GOD, and my life experience. On top of that, my inner critic reminded me that I was a high school dropout, an unwed mother, often entangled in turbulent relationships, burdened with a negative attitude, and had a history of drug use.

In my mind, there was no way that GOD could use someone like me, particularly in ministry. Yet despite my resistance, GOD continued to pursue and accost me. Let me tell you something—GOD has a permissive will, which means GOD gives you and me the free will to choose our path. That's very good news for a woman named Melvina, who doesn't like anyone telling her what to do, and that includes GOD... until now. Having the right to choose is both a gift and a responsibility.

Due to fear, I resisted being called a preacher. Instead, I called myself an inspirational speaker. GOD said, It does not matter what you call yourself, Ms. Melvina. GOD reminded me that I was called to carry a very simple message of recovery and redemption. By the power of GOD, Jesus Christ, the Holy Spirit, and the Twelve-Steps of Narcotics Anonymous, my life was restored.

The truth is, since childhood, I have always loved talking—and I still do because I have something to say. My mother used to joke that I talked more than the radio. LOL!

I'm cracking up just thinking about that! Perhaps, I was practicing to be an orator, a preacher, or an inspirational speaker. When I started preaching, I said to my mother, Well, now we know why I talked so much as a child! And we laughed together. Such precious memories.

Not long after GOD called me to preach, my first pastor, at Grace Baptist Church of Christ (GBCOC) in East New York, Brooklyn, allowed me to preach on one of the Seven Last Words of Christ. I was not licensed to preach at that time. I started attending GBCOC in early recovery, and I even got married there. Believe or not, I had less than 90 days clean when I got married.

During the wonder/wander years, I attended bible study and midweek services faithfully, I led a Girl Scouts troop, I sang in the choir, and I served as a missionary. Imagine me in that white uniform—white stockings, white shoes, and that white doily perched on my head. LOL! That uniform certainly cramped my style, but I was serious about changing my life. I did whatever was necessary to embrace a new way of living.

I was always ready and prepared for bible study, because I genuinely wanted to learn about GOD. My opinions about the Scriptures, about Jesus, about GOD, and other religious matters often differed from those of the other members, including the pastor. He would often say to me "I want to see you in my office to discuss your ideas." He tried to persuade me to adopt his point of view, which I appreciated. I have my own understanding of religion, GOD, and life, and I have never allowed anyone to force me into their way of thinking.

Somewhere around 1994, I left that church to become a member at Universal Baptist Church (UBC) in Bedford Stuyvesant. My sponsor was involved with a ministry made up of individuals who had overcome addiction. We traveled to various churches, and we even came to Richmond, VA to testify about how GOD brought us out of darkness into His marvelous light (1 Peter 2:9).

While I was a member at UBC, I participated in their Bible institute, which deepened my desire to learn more about GOD. I enrolled in the New York School of the Bible in Manhattan, where I earned a certificate.

In 1998, I joined St. Paul Community Baptist Church in East New York, Brooklyn. While there, I was involved with the children's ministry. That was not my calling, but I was willing to serve. The ministry was robust and meaningful, and the drama ministry was phenomenal. There were so many gifted women and men involved. The pastor made it clear that he was not called to license women. Cool. At the time his statement did not affect me, because I had not yet fully embraced GOD's call on my life, nor was I ready to be licensed or ordained. I did not perceive his opinion as misogyny then, and I still do not see it that way now. What I know for sure was that GOD called me to preach, not man. I remained at that church until I moved to RVA in 2001.

Several brilliant professors taught at VUU including my homiletics (preaching) professor, whose teaching style I admired. I visited and joined his church, Second Baptist Church (SBC) in the Randolph community. My pastor recognized my gift for biblical interpretation (hermeneutics), and encouraged me to pursue a doctorate in preaching, though I wasn't interested at the time. I served in various ministries including the women's ministry, preaching regularly, pastoral counseling, and the Congregational Needs Committee. He also gave me opportunities in worship leadership, teaching Bible study, assisting with baptisms, weddings, funerals, and other church events.

My pastor recognized my teaching and preaching gifts. At the time, I was actively involved in ministry at local jails and prisons, conducting personal development workshops for incarcerated women. During my residency as a chaplain at Virginia Commonwealth University Health Systems (VCUHS), I requested assignment to the ward for incarcerated patients. Impressed by my passion and dedication, my pastor decided to license and ordain me to the gospel ministry.

In 2005, during a conversation with a coworker, she connected me by phone with a woman she knew. I don't recall what prompted the connections, but the woman on the phone invited me to Love Outreach Ministries (LOM), and I agreed to go. Mind you, the woman who had invited me didn't show up that Sunday. I sat through the service captivated by the preacher's fervor and knowledge about GOD. After the service, I introduced myself only to discover that she was the pastor. During our initial conversation, we felt an immediate connection, and before long, she became my mentor. Both of us believed that GOD had used the anonymous woman to bring us together.

Not only was the church led by a woman, but she was also the visionary and founder of LOM. I knew that women pastored churches, but it was rare. The pastor was a woman of small stature—under five feet tall— but her faith was gigantic. A short time after we met, she prophesied that I would one day be her successor as pastor. Whoa! WOW! That was completely unexpected. You can bet I was shaking in my boots.

The pastor consistently testified about GOD's goodness and the many blessings GOD showered on her. About a year after I joined the church, one of her spiritual daughters returned from the military. We got along well, but there seemed to be some jealousy and competition between us. In general, I am not naturally a competitive person, so I chose to leave the church. It did not matter to me that I was stepping away from the blessing my pastor had imparted to me. When we discussed the situation, she assured me that all would be well, but I lacked the patience to hold on.

During the summer of 2011, I returned to LOM, but by that time Pastor was very ill. The young lady who previously returned from the military was no longer at the church. Pastor once again passed the pastoral mantle to me, and I graciously accepted it. In addition to preaching, weekly Bible study and Sunday worship, I established an addiction ministry offering a 12-step Bible study every Saturday. The ministry began to flourish and thrive. Around July 2012, Pastor blessed me with a lump sum of money. Initially, I refused it, but she gently insisted that I accept it. When I informed the overseer, who also happened to be her son—he accused me of manipulation and taking advantage of the Pastor's medical condition. I humbly returned the money, though Pastor was not pleased with my decision, nor was she pleased with her son's interference in her financial affairs. Despite this incident, I remained at the church though the relationship with the overseer became strained. I stayed in my position, ready to fulfill my purpose as a preacher and a pastor, even though I was still somewhat uncomfortable with it.

A few months later, after a long fight with health issues. I had the honor of eulogizing and celebrating a life well lived. Although I deeply missed my pastor, I continued to develop the ministry. The church members were enthusiastic about doing community-based ministry. However, during the planning stage, the overseer was not supportive of church growth. A few days before Thanksgiving in 2013, he dismissed me from the pastorate. My, my, my— I was crushed, hurt, angry, and embarrassed. In essence, he evicted me from the church. Even now, when I reflect on that incident, it still causes me to wince. The experience left a very bitter taste in my mouth. I was not angry with GOD or with the universal church; I was angry with the overseer. That was one of the most traumatic experiences of my life.

A couple of years ago, while working the 8th step with my sponsor, it became clear that I owed amends to some of the congregations that loved, supported, and affirmed me. In the Basic Text of Narcotics Anonymous, the eight-step reads this way: *"We made a list of all persons we had harmed, and became willing to make amends to them all"* (p.37).

Thankfully, I was able to make direct amends to my pastor at SBC for being dismissive, not taking my call seriously, and for my decision to leave the ministry abruptly. When I become aware of a shortcoming or a character defect, I usually take personal responsibility and ownership of my actions. However, before working the 8th Step, it never occurred to me that the people who are associated with those organizations were affected by my walking away, particularly when I left without saying 'so long.' One of my shortcomings is that I tend to lock onto an idea, and once the thought is lodged in my mind, off to the races I go.

As a seasoned woman, I am more apt to think my decisions through before acting on them, than I was in the past. I declare war on those old, negative ways of being and doing. I am no longer a slave to the rhythms of yesteryear or yesterday. Until now I was afraid of GOD's goodness, but as I have gained wisdom, it has become easier to accept that GOD has great things in store for me. Yet, in order to receive them, it is imperative to give GOD a full yes even though doubt and fear continue to assail me.

As I have said before, I believe that the word purpose is not singular. Since 2013, I have had the privilege of teaching at a local community college in Richmond, Virginia, my second love—teaching—while dancing remains my first. I began as an adjunct professor, and in October 2024, I was offered a full-time professor position at the same college. It is truly amazing how GOD has orchestrated my life, even when I have drifted from time to time. I'll say it again: don't lose heart on the journey to becoming you. The best is yet to come. Remember, no experience is wasted or lost in GOD's kingdom. Keep the faith.

CLEVER (Brilliance)

Did you know that brilliance is a gift from GOD? Some of us, myself included, have been guilty of shrinking ourselves to fit in. We fear our own brilliance and cleverness, but I am talking about me. At age nine, my mother told me that I was smart and ambitious. Now, I didn't know exactly what ambitious meant, but it sure sounded important. Early in life, my mother saw my potential; she affirmed it, and continued to affirm it throughout her life. Whenever one of her children, grandchildren and so on accomplished a goal, one of her favorite sayings was "You've just put another jewel in my crown." I've jokingly said, "Ma, that crown should be really heavy by now," but in her quick wit, she retorted, "My crown is never too heavy." She strutted and wore her crown as proudly as a peacock. My mother went on to glory on August 20, 2023 at the ripe age of 96. May her affirmations never be forgotten, for they are life-giving, continually reminding me of who I am, what I am, and whose I am.

Please remember: do not dumb yourself down. Stop playing small and shrinking yourself to fit in to please others. In this world, so many of us strive for sameness, instead of trusting in our GOD given brilliance. Now, please don't get me wrong—we need people on this journey. Remember when we talked about your community of believers as a support system? Join me in refusing to be a carbon copy of anyone, and refuse to be pigeonholed into a certain way of being, thinking, or doing.

CLEAR

Earlier in this book, we identified the chitchat (inner critic) that can potentially hinder our progress. Now that you know what your "chitchat" is, SHUT IT UP, Melvina (put your name here). How do you SHUT IT UP, you ask? Just tell it to SHUT UP! You have the power to change the course of your thinking, but you must pay attention to your thoughts in order to transform them. In 12-step circles we call it *stinking thinking*.

Practice changing the chitchat in your mind. You know what I am talking about, right? Those conversations with yourself—where you listen to and agree with the voices that tell you that what you desire is not possible because... fill in the blank.

It is essential to listen to your chitchat otherwise you won't be able to develop strategies to silence the noise in your head. The goal is to silence the chitchat and replace it with affirmative prayer, meditation, kind words, uplifting music and other things that motivate you toward your goals and aspirations.

Remember: what you think about, you bring about. Pay close attention to your thoughts, your behaviors, and your attitudes. Your primary responsibility through this process is to be a gatekeeper—of your thoughts, your words, your actions, and ultimately your life. If it is to be, it is up to you. Say it with me three times: If it is to be, it is up to ME. If it is to be, it is up to ME. If it is to be, it is up to ME. Make this your personal mantra.

Replace the "chitchat" with positive affirmations. You're probably thinking, here she goes with positive affirmations, and I get it I feel the same way. However, when we fail to counter self-defeating thoughts with affirmations, we surrender our authority to a lower power, making it much harder to stay committed to our vision. If affirmations don't work for you, find something that does, and use it consistently.

CHARTING YOUR COURSE

We have been having a lot of meaningful conversations, and that will continue as we navigate twists and turns on this journey called life. Back in 2011, I developed a life journey diagram that was designed to help me gain self-understanding and self-acceptance. As I've shared before, I am on a quest to know and accept the fullness of who I am in the present moment.

I believe each of us is a hero in our own right. How else could we have made it through the challenging situations and circumstances we faced? Heroes fail and succeed, fail and succeed, and fail and succeed, over and over again—but they continue moving forward despite it all. In the process of falling and rising, we accumulate battle scars and beauty marks. I've gotten quite dirty from living life on life's terms, yet I keep on pushing to see what lies ahead. I truly believe—and firmly contend that GOD does GOD's best work in dirt (Genesis 3).

The image below is a life journey chart that I created of my life a few years ago. At the center, I see the one-year-old Melvina—a little girl brimming with hidden talent. That little girl had no idea what life had in store for her, yet she already looks like a force to be reckoned with. My parents and siblings often reminded me of my curiosity. One of my brothers loves to tell the story about a genie lamp we found, which I would rub repeatedly to see if it had magical powers, LOL!

THE LIFE JOURNEY: CHARTNG YOUR COURSE

A	B	C	D	E	F
G	H	I	J	K	L
M	N	O	P	Q	R
S	T	U	V	W	X
Y	Z	1	2	3	4
5	6	7	8	9	0
?	,	=	$	%	.

 9/2011

Let me explain the Life Journey Chart. On the diagram are the alphabet, numbers, punctuation marks, and symbols. For this discussion, let's say that A (teacher/preacher) is GOD's purpose for my life. To become A, I have to experience various things for my perosnal growth and development. So I venture to B (school), then I go to C (library). As my excitement grows and 1 begin to delve into various experiences, I saunter to D (my first boyfriend at age 16). By age 20, I'm at E, and I've accumulated various experiences, good, bad, and indifferent, and on and on it goes. Simply put, the life journey chart is designed to help us to see how we move through life. My chart helped me to see how situations and circumstances contributed to me becoming who I am today. In the recovery process, Step 4 helped assist me to identify and reconcile the wreckage or the dirt of my past. Step 4 reads: *"We made a searching and fearless moral inventory of ourselves."*

The dirt consists of my failures, my decision-making, shame, guilt, achievements, promotions, and so on. In the past, my perceived failure caused me to think that it was useless to continue on a certain path. On this fantastic voyage called life, I have pursued alternate routes when I got discouraged or bored. For example, instead of accepting that I am a preacher, I pursued motivational/inspirational speaking, life coaching, etc. I ignored GOD's purpose and plan because in my mind, I didn't measure up to the traditional standard of a preacher, so I found an alternate route.

From my nomadic perspective, GOD does GOD's best work in dirt, the dirt being the experiences we have had throughout our life span. I have wandered off course countless times, and it has not changed GOD's mind about me yet. Every experience and encounter I have had is purposeful. There are no wasted moments or experiences. I believe my inconsistencies, choices, decisions, derailments, detours, and distractions are all designed to craft a better me. The biblical text Jeremiah 18:1-10 (NIV) is a prime example of charting my course. It reads: "This is the word that came to Jeremiah from the Lord: ²'Go down to the potter's house, and there I will give you my message.' ³So I went down to the potter's house, and I saw him working at the wheel. ⁴But the pot he was shaping from the clay was marred in his hands; so the potter formed it into another pot, shaping it as seemed best to him."

If you know anything about pottery, then you know that it's a multi-step process that takes time. A potter needs certain materials, tools, and appliances to produce a masterpiece. Imagine the potter mixing various ingredients to design a masterpiece, YOU. Ingredients such as your parents, your birthplace, your birthdate, your personality, your vocation, and your destiny, to name a few things. Verse 4 reads:

⁴But the pot he was shaping from the clay was marred in his hands; so, the potter formed it into another pot, shaping it as seemed best to him."

The way the verse is written, it appears that there was something wrong with the potter's hand, but remember, GOD is a master potter. The pot seems to have experienced some issues while in the potter's hand. The truth of the matter is that you and I often get off of the potter's wheel before GOD is finished with us. Let's be clear, there wasn't anything wrong with the potter's hand, the issue was with the clay (me & you). Trials and tribulations can alter my perception, which can result in me feeling like a failure. Some of us silently blame GOD and other people for the way our lives turned out. Of course, you would not dare to blame GOD aloud, or would you? GOD can handle your accusations. Try it and see.

One of the appliances a potter uses is a kiln, which is like a furnace. I don't know about you, but I have been in some heated situations that caused me to faint under the flames. Over the years, I discovered that my failures, my foul-ups, and my fumbles were designed to make me stronger, to develop my faith, to build my character, and ultimately to trust GOD. In the bible, in John 16:33, Jesus said, "In this life you will have tribulation." Tribulation like a pandemic, abandonment issues, neglect, addiction, mental and medical conditions, grief & loss, trauma, divorce, and unemployment, etc., etc. The good news is that through the fumes, the fuel, and the fire, all of us are in GOD's care and GOD's hands. We can trust the master potter. GOD is so masterful and intentional that every life experience is purposefully worked into the clay for my good and for your good, too. Those things are my testimony, my story, which will bring GOD glory.

GOD, the master potter has a way of repurposing the fragments and fractures of our lives, particularly when we seemingly wander off course. In the past, I used to criticize myself for not trusting GOD's plan for my life. On so many occasions, GOD whispered to me, 'Melvina, stop worrying and condemning yourself. Don't you know that you are still in my care, and I love you no matter what you do or don't do.' I have come to understand that GOD does not tell me what the process of becoming will be. GOD tends to give the vision of what we are to become or to do, with very little detail. I suppose that if I had known the outcome in advance, I would have missed the journey to becoming the woman that I am. I am learning to not fret over things and to trust GOD even when I don't know the whole process. GOD knows that I enjoy stepping out on faith, and I also thrive on taking uncalculated risks. I am learning that the things that I consider as failures, GOD views as fodder for the masterpiece. It is refreshing to know that I did not fumble GOD's plan for my life despite giving up at times.

Now, when I peer into the mirror, I still see some of the things I've gone through, but GOD has masterfully blended and kneaded them into this beautiful woman that I am proud of. No longer am I fighting against GOD's plans (as much), especially since I will not win the tug-of-war with GOD. Jeremiah 29:11 (NIV) asserts: "For I know the plans I have for you, declares the LORD, plans to prosper you and not to harm you, plans to give you hope and a future." I see one of your wings coming out of the cocoon. Come out, come out and soar you beautiful butterfly.

CLEARING THE HEART

Forgiveness is a cleansing and clearing balm that is essential to our spiritual growth and development. I hear your thoughts from here. Some of you are saying, she must be crazy if she thinks I'm going to FORGIVE so and so for what they did to me. Well, call me crazy if that's what it takes for you to at least consider forgiveness. Hopefully, your consideration will evolve into a willingness to use the F Word. Again, I say, it's time to FORGIVE. FORGIVENESS is a part of the clearing process. Matthew 18:21-22 (KJV) states: "Then came Peter to Jesus and said, Lord, how often shall my brother sin against me and I forgive him? As many as seven times? Jesus said to him. "I do not say to you seven times, but seventy times seven."

In essence, Jesus taught a spiritual truth that can potentially set us free from ourselves as well as from the past. Forgiveness is an ongoing process. It is not a one-shot deal, or a one-and-done kind of thing. Although GOD forgives us when we ask for it, forgiveness is more than feeling relieved. Forgiveness is a state of being. Upon investigation, I discovered that forgiveness is like a laxative (Ex-Lax or Citric

Magnesia). I remember the days when my mother gave my siblings and me an Ex-Lax every month. The purpose of taking a laxative is to clean your system out. Think about it: Have you ever been constipated? Do you recall how you felt? It is one of the most miserable feelings because when you're constipated, it is difficult to think; you don't want to eat or talk. All you want to do is move your bowels to eliminate waste from your body. From a spiritual perspective, some of us are constipated with the issues of life from our past and present realities. Jesus offered Peter a spiritual laxative in the form of forgiveness. Once the body has extracted the nutrients from food, the rest of it becomes waste. Holding onto physical and spiritual waste can result in feelings of inertia, lethargy, and stagnation. Forgiveness provides a doorway to let go of resentments, bitterness, anger, abuse, etc. Right here and right now, you can release those character defects and shortcomings into the abyss or the sea of forgetfulness. Hopefully, you can see how vital forgiveness is for your overall well-being and total peace.

Forgiveness is a gift that GOD gave us to use as a healing balm to change our lives. Forgiveness is not about the other person. Forgiveness does not excuse or nullify the behavior or conduct of other people. Not at all. Forgiveness sets you free. YES YOU! You do want to be free, right? I thought so. Well then, let's start the journey toward healing. Are you coming? Philippians 4:13 (NIV) declares: "I can do all things through Christ who gives me strength." Here's how it works. When you think about the people who have hurt you, violated you, disappointed you, abandoned you, and/or betrayed you, etc.

Instead of allowing people to live rent-free in your mind, use the F word (forgiveness) to change the course of your life. Say this with me: I forgive you (name the person, institution, organization, or situation). I forgive myself for (fill in the blank). Instead of engaging in condemnation, decide to bless yourself and others by recognizing the importance of changing your language and choosing to forgive. Trust and believe that you have the power within yourself to let go of people, places, and things that have hurt or harmed you. Simply put, you have to decide to forgive. Deuteronomy 30:19 (KJV) says: "I call heaven and earth to record this day against you, that I have set before you, life and death, blessing and cursing: therefore choose life that both you and your seed may live."

CEASE

Good job on the forgiveness work you just did. I knew you could do it. I hope you're feeling good about yourself. If you haven't taken the forgiveness step yet, that's okay too. In Matt 17:21, Jesus said, "This kind only comes out through prayer and fasting." Take some time to CEASE right now. Yes, I mean it; CEASE. While forgiveness is freeing, forgiveness can cause you to feel exhausted and depleted, which is normal. Remember, you are clearing the path for your vision to come into fruition. Remind yourself that you are resilient, and that you can bounce back better than before. GOD deposited inner strength and wisdom in you at birth. Tap into the power of GOD within you. If you are feeling spiritually, emotionally, mentally, and/or physically exhausted, take time to CEASE, but return within 24 hours to continue the journey.

Just be with yourself right now. Let go of everything. Put the chores aside. Let go of self-defeating thoughts. Let go of people, places, and things that don't serve you. Let go of the anger. Let go of the past. Let go of expectations. Let go of aspirations. Simply let go. Allow yourself to be in this present moment. Suspend all judgment and desires at this time. BREATHE! LET GO!

I am reminded of the time when I was employed as a substance abuse counselor at a women's residential treatment center in Richmond, VA. One day, as I listened to individuals share about the issues that contributed to their addiction, the notion 'SO WHAT ' came to mind, and before I knew it, the words SO WHAT organically escaped from my mouth. The expression on the client's faces was priceless. Initially, they were in utter shock, but based on my relationship with them, I trusted the process. I didn't say 'SO WHAT to minimize anything that the women shared about; I said 'SO WHAT to open an authentic dialogue about the things that tend to bog us down. I intended to shine a light on the blame game that we often engage in. We certainly have the right to be downright angry and upset about the neglect, abandonment, betrayal, verbal, sexual, and physical abuse, and so on, we endured at the hands of people who claimed to love us. The purpose of saying 'SO WHAT' allows us to take the power and sting out of the things that were designed to destroy and hurt us. I dare you to look at your past, and boldly and courageously declare 'SO WHAT'. That's right, just say 'SO WHAT' when the past rears its head. Silence the chit-chat and say 'SO WHAT'. Practice saying SO WHAT daily, and you will discover that what others meant for evil, GOD will turn it around to work to your advantage (Genesis 50). As a result of saying SO WHAT during the group process, one of the participants still addresses me as SO WHAT whenever we see one another, which makes both of us giggle.

CIRCLES (Labyrinth)

Have you ever felt like you are going around and around in circles? Well I have, so welcome to the club of feeling a sense of chaos and confusion. There are times in my life when I have felt tangled, jumbled and knotted in my body, my mind and my spirit, and the truth be told, I still experience it from time to time. I have come to understand that life ebbs and flows; that what goes around comes around.

One of the tools that has helped me throughout my recovery journey is the labyrinth. A labyrinth is an ancient structure that consists of circles and spirals that meander from one point to another, leading you to the center. It is often found in parks and religious institutions. It can be used for spiritual growth and development. Although the labyrinth resembles a maze, it is not a maze. The journey through a labyrinth is symbolic of life's twists and turns. In essence, the labyrinth represents a sacred journey. I wholeheartedly believe that the answers to life are within me (us). Whenever I experience indecisiveness or confusion, I go to the labyrinth to meditate and pray to gain clarity, courage, self-discovery, and transformation etc. The answer does not always come right away, but just the simple act of walking in circles has the potential to untangle me from the inside out, providing a sense of release and relief. Walking the labyrinth occurs externally, but it is both an internal and external experience. Chances are there is a labyrinth somewhere in your city. For more information, visit: https://labyrinthsociety.org

CRY/CATHARSIS

Sometimes when I walk the labyrinth, I have experienced AHA moments, and other times it brings me to tears. Did you know that tears are a gift? I know, I know; big girls don't cry, and men don't have the right to cry, or so we have been taught to believe. That is all a lie. From a metaphysical standpoint, when I repress and suppress my emotions, I cause harm to myself in more ways than one. The NA Basic Text says: "We did many people great harm, but most of all we harmed ourselves (p. 13).

When I say metaphysically, I mean that pent-up emotions can attack our internal organs, which in turn can contribute to medical issues such as pulmonary disorders, mental health disorders, high blood pressure, diabetes, various cancers, and the list goes on.

Disclaimer: The metaphysical comment is my personal opinion, not a medical one. Please consult your healthcare professional about your medical and mental health conditions.

As I write this book, there is a heavy weight pressing on my total being. I keep telling myself that I need a good cry, but I can't make myself cry. I need a cleansing, a clearing, a cathartic type of cry. On a couple of occasions, I have experienced cathartic moments whereby I broke down in uncontrollable tears. When that happened, the tears came out of nowhere; It has happened at home, in public, at work, and in a social setting. What I do recall about those moments is that right before they happened, I was dealing with some kind of stress in my life, which was job-related, issues in a romantic relationship, financial distress, and/or spiritual unrest.

Crying allows us to release pent-up energy. One day, during my morning walk, it dawned on me that crying brings clarity. Crying gives us power. Crying allows GOD to enter in with us. Crying allows you to surrender your thoughts, your emotions, and your feelings in the moment. Come on now, you know you want to cry. Like me, you have probably been wanting to cry for a long time. Tears are cleansing. You and I don't need a reason to cry. When the tears come without your permission, allow them to nurture you and to bathe you. Just cry for the sake of crying. The psalmist in Psalm 42:3 (NIV) adequately declared: "My tears have been my food day and night, while all day long people say to me, 'Where is your God?'"

When the tears come, allow them to flow naturally. Make every effort to refrain from using tissue or accepting tissue from others if you are in the presence of people. In my experience, tissue and water are distractions, and they interrupt the healing process. Unfortunately, many of us are good at cutting off our emotions, I know I am. But if we truly want to heal from the inside out, sometimes an ugly cry is exactly what our spirits need. Let the tears, the snot, and the slobber flow. I know an ugly cry can be embarrassing, but allow yourself the gift of releasing your tears. Take as much time as you need. This is a time to release the old so that you can be restored, and find a new way to live your life on purpose. Allow the tears to naturally dry on the canvas of your face. Journal about your experience, if you so desire, to capture this pivotal moment in your journey.

CLEANSE

After a cathartic release, a warm bath can rejuvenate, reinvigorate, and reenergize your spirit. Gather your fragrant oils, soft towels, cozy loungewear, and a glass of water or your favorite beverage to drink. Sink into the tub with water at a comfortable temperature, and allow yourself to unwind. Whether you pick up a book, explore new treatments online, or simply find your own way to refresh your mind, body, and spirit, embrace the moment as an act of self-love. Take a moment to hug yourself and honor the beautiful person you are. As you soak, release negativity into the water. When you are ready, remain in the tub as it drains, imagining your burdens and cares flowing away with the water. As you rise from the bath you emerge renewed with a fresh sense of hope, faith, and purpose. Allow your skin to dry naturally, savoring the moment. And, if baths aren't for you, a shower can be just as cleansing and restorative.

In addition to cleansing the physical body with water, intermittent fasting is good for the soul, too. Fasting is also good for clearing your mind, your body, and your spirit. There are many types of fasts. Traditionally, people fasted food, but there are some creative ways to fast too. Some people fast unwanted attitudes, habits, and behaviors. Such as your favorite television show, overeating, gossiping, smoking, shopping, etc. You decide what, when, and how long. There are all sorts of theories about how long it takes to break a habit, but ultimately, all change begins with a decision followed by action. The Living Clean: The Journey Continues asserts: "Willingness without action is fantasy" (p.197). I agree with that wholeheartedly. Action is the driving force that kicks my willingness into gear. Remember to drink plenty of water daily to hydrate your body.

Disclaimer: Taking a bath and fasting are my personal opinions not a medical one. Please consult your healthcare professional if you have conditions that prevent you from immersing in water, using certain products or engaging in any type of fasting.

CLEAN

When was the last time you engaged in a deep cleaning of your home? When my living space is disorganized, it affects my spiritual, emotional and mental well-being. You might be feeling perplexed because you don't know where to start, right? That is normal. We often get overwhelmed when it comes to getting organized and discarding stuff.

Some of us remember the good old days when our parents cleaned the house for holidays and special occasions. Go ahead, move the furniture from the walls and chase out those dust mites. Oh look, is that the pair of shoes I've been looking for under the couch? I was wondering where they'd gone. Now that's worth a laugh!!!

If you come across items that belong in another room, set them aside in a basket or bag, and move them once you've finished cleaning the current room. Even better keep a basket or a plastic bag in the room so you can quickly deposit misplaced items and avoid getting sidetracked and distracted. Once you're done, take the receptacle and return the items to their proper places. Remember to stay focused; complete the task before moving on. Here is a suggested way to go about cleaning/clearing your space.

- Develop an action plan. Keep it simple.

- Decide which room you want to start with. You DO NOT have to clean the entire space in one day, but if you choose to do so, that is your choice.

- Plan to clean/clear one room at a time. In the rooms of Twelve-Step recovery we have some nice one-liners such as "Easy Does It", and I'll add "But do it."

- Wash window treatments, blankets, shampoo carpet, wax floors, etc.

- You can turn cleaning into a party. Invite your friends over to help.

- Solicit the help of your children. Offer them a reward for helping.

- Hire a cleaning service if you can afford it.

- Add plants to oxygenate and purify the air.

- Get rid of household and clothing items you no longer need. It can definitely be tough. I don't know about you, but I am holding on to clothes and footwear that I can no longer fit or better yet, that are out of style, but I just can't seem to let them go. I'm working on it. For real though. LOL!

- Plan an event with family and friends to exchange and/or give away unwanted items. A few years ago, my daughter and her friends got together and exchanged unwanted items. They called it "New to Me," which is a clever way to get rid of things that no longer serve you.

CREATE

This is the fun part. Below are several suggestions to create the life you want. You can select one, you can do them all, or you can choose not to do them at all; it's entirely up to you. Your life is not an assignment. Please, please, please don't pressure yourself. Remember, this is a journey or a quest, not a marathon. The journey within is unparalleled by any other. In a real sense, the journey within is an adventure, an odyssey, or a fantastic voyage, as I like to call it. You will discover all sorts of things about yourself. Remember, easy does it, but do it! I love the song by *Lakeside, Fantastic Voyage (1980)*. Listen to it when you get a moment.

- Vision Board – A vision board is a creative way to display your goals and aspirations. You can create the life you want with words, images, magazine clippings, etc. Purchase poster board, glue sticks, crayons, scissors, and other craft items. Be as creative as you choose, just make sure that your vision board is posted where you can see it daily. Once it's completed, take a picture with your device so you will have it with you at all times to remind yourself of your goals.

- Montage – When I was in seminary at Virginia Union University (VUU), one of my professors taught a class titled 'Sacred Self.' In that class, the students were expected to tell their life story through creative means. I decided to create a montage. A montage is a collection of pictures that reflects a timeline of one's life. A montage differs from a collage, which is an assembly of images pasted on a surface in no particular order. I invite you to gather pictures of yourself, from early childhood to the present day if you have them. You'll discover that this exercise can guide you on an inward journey. As you work on this project, you may notice peaks and valleys in your life. Most importantly, I hope you will see how you have grown and developed physically, emotionally, spiritually, and mentally over your life span.

When I created my montage in 2003, it was very affirming, and it propelled me forward to accomplish my aspirations. By looking at pictures from the past, I was able to re-experience the good old days, as well as some of the days of yesteryear that were challenging. In essence, I learned to appreciate and honor myself. In hindsight, I realize that GOD used every single incident, circumstance, and situation from the day I was born to the present day to develop my character, and to shape me into the woman that I am becoming.

- Timeline – This is an interesting exercise. Traditionally, timelines were used to record historical events, but your life is a historical record too. A timeline can illustrate the ebb and flow of your life experiences. The pictures you gather can help jog your memory about dates or periods in your life that you may have long forgotten. Your timeline can also reveal how events, situations, and circumstances are connected. What you choose to include is entirely up to you. The goal is to document and reflect on your life, helping you gain self-understanding as you move toward the life you desire.

- Genogram – On your quest of self-discovery, exploring your family tree can provide valuable insight. A genogram is a diagram of your maternal and paternal families that highlights relationship dynamics, career or education paths, trauma, mental health, drug addiction, health issues, and communication styles, and more. Talk with family members to learn about your family of origin. If you don't know your biological family due to abandonment, foster care or adoption, or death, create the genogram based on the environment in which you were raised. Remember, these are simple exercises designed to help you understand yourself better. Please don't abandon yourself, just keep it moving. Resources like Ancestry.com can also assist in tracing your family history.

CHOOSING TO BREATHE

It's time to BREATHE. Maybe you're hearing that old familiar voice again saying this is too much to do, I don't feel like it, or I'm tired; I think I'll take a nap. Shut down the "CHIT-CHAT." Or maybe you feel exhilarated and full of energy. Whichever place you find yourself in right now, it's time to BREATHE. I encourage you to honor your feelings, but make sure to return to your creative exercise.

- Mindfulness – Find a quiet comfortable space and get in a posture that helps you to relax, reorient and rejuvenate. BREATHE deeply inhaling through your nose. Hold your breath for a few seconds and then slowly exhale the energy/toxins from your mouth. Repeat several times. When you are ready, return to the exercises or do something fun that you enjoy.

- If you need to nap, feel free to do so because napping can refresh and renew your spirit. Before taking the next step, it is imperative to spend quality time with yourself and with GOD. Go ahead, I dare you to find

something fun to do that you enjoy. Maybe you need
to clown around. LOL!

93

CLOWN (Circus, Comedy, etc.)

Let's have fun for a change. You like that, huh? Me too. Fun can be a powerful catalyst for change. Have you ever watched children at play? They are naturally curious about their environment, and remarkably fearless. Let's reconnect with the child within us and embrace that same curiosity. Self-discovery doesn't have to be arduous or overly serious. We can enjoy the journey as we grow into the person we aspire to become.

With that said, this activity requires you to get out of your comfort zone. Being serious is a part of my nature, so there is no judgment here. Fellow traveler, please put that to-do list aside for now. Let's learn how to create a to-be list instead. As I write this, I'm reminded of that part of me that loves to laugh. Me, myself, and I love to laugh. As a child, I was very silly. Whenever I told a funny story, it was difficult to get to the punchline because I was laughing before I even got there. I miss that part of myself, and it's a very significant part that I'm working to reclaim. Do you have any joy juice? Joy juice is what allows us to laugh at ourselves. I laugh at myself often, because, well, sometimes I am a little bit cray

cray. For those who don't know what cray cray is, it's urban language for crazy. Laughing my butt off (LMBO)!

95

CLOWNING CONSIDERATIONS

Give yourself the gift of fun. Clowning isn't about digesting or processing information. It's about pure fun. Dance with yourself, play hopscotch, jump rope, whatever brings you joy. Just have fun without an agenda. Purchase tickets to a comedy show, the circus, or a magic show. No serious discussions, just pure unadulterated, unapologetic silliness and fun. Let those endorphins flow and release your stress. Regular laughter can reduce stress much like crying does. All we need is to free ourselves from the internal messages that tell us we're too old for this or that. Proverbs 17:22 says it this way: "Laughter and merriment are good medicine for the soul, but a broken spirit saps a person's strength." You deserve to laugh, and you need to laugh. Go for it. Give a hoot, a snicker, a chuckle.

CAREFREE

Wasn't clowning marvelous; Simply marvelous, eh? We need more of that and less of the things that cause stress. Take a moment to sit back and reflect on how you felt while clowning. Journal if you please. Make it a practice to do something fun regularly and rediscover your playful side. Rediscover your fun side. In 1983, Cyndi Lauper reminded us: Girls Just Wanna Have Fun, and men do too. All work and no play makes life dull. So go on and do your thang, but don't hurt anyone, including yourself, okay. LOL!

CLOSE

I heard of a wise woman who made it a point to end each day with what she called a 'Zip in the day'. Putting a zip in the day was a way of ending the day with fun and finality. Putting a zip in the day is to say that no matter what happened today, I choose to end my day on a positive note. Putting a zip in the day can be something as simple as drinking mint julep tea, taking a relaxing bath, reading a novel, and/or calling an old friend. It's anything you want it to be. Go for it; you deserve it and so much more.

Lastly, try to end the day with journaling, prayer, and/or meditation. Prayer can serve as powerful ammunition against the inner critic. Many of us grew up with parents, grandparents, or relatives who required us to kneel beside the bed to offer a prayer of thanksgiving for our parents, our loved ones, the world at large, and our toys LOL! Can you believe I stopped praying at night some time ago? No wonder I began losing direction and the ability to realize my aspirations. I've since realized that the unconscious choice to stop praying regularly gave the enemy a foothold in my life.

A good friend shared that she opens and ends the day with prayer. What a good idea. After that conversation with my friend, I started a nightly practice to pray again before retiring. Kneeling is a little challenging for this seasoned saint, because these knees are not meant for kneeling anymore. It can be challenging to get up off of my knees. Imagine me scuffling to get up; bracing myself this way and that way to get up, so I've learned to sit in a chair or simply lie down in bed to pray and meditate. Sometimes I fall asleep during the process, but at least I arrived in la-la land while talking to GOD. I hear you laughing at me, and I am laughing too. In a nutshell, however you choose to pray, find what works for you.

COMMITMENT/CONSISTENCY

If you're anything like me, committing to something can trigger anxiety and fear. Some of us fear commitment because we have been scarred emotionally, physically, and mentally at the hands of those we loved and trusted. Others were taught to commit to people, places, and things at the expense of themselves. We commit to intimate relationships, to family, friends, employers, and so on. Still others of us struggle with feelings of inadequacy, insecurity, and insignificance. But remember: GOD qualifies us; we don't have to qualify ourselves. How about giving yourself what you so readily give to others? Commitment is one of the hardest things to do. However, commitment without consistency has often fallen flat for me. Commitment means to dedicate, promise, or pledge to do something. Consistency means steadiness, regularity, stability, a stick-to-itiveness. For me consistency is more fitting. We each have to define what is consistent for ourselves, not what others expect it to be. Consistency allows us to keep trying, even when it's difficult or unpleasant.

Commitment and consistency are still very challenging for me. Fighting the inner me, the inner critic, the self-doubt, the spiritual ADHD, the resistance, and so on is all challenging. Excuse me for a moment. It is time for me to CEASE and breathe. It feels like a breakthrough, a breakdown, and a breakup with mediocrity all at once. Oh my GOD, thank you for bringing this to my awareness. As I write this book, I constantly combat the voices that say "I don't feel like it or I'm tired." My fellow spiritual sojourners, I repeat: fighting the inner critic is no easy feat. I probably said this elsewhere, but it bears repeating.

Disclaimer: The words that follow reflect my personal experience. I do not have the authority to diagnose anyone, nor am I attempting to do so. I am not suggesting that you, the reader, have spiritual malaise, mental health disorders or any medical conditions. Please consult your healthcare professional or primary care physician if you require professional assistance.

Many of us have heard of attention deficit hyperactivity disorder (ADHD). Growing up, I was never diagnosed with ADHD; however, as an adult, I consider myself to have spiritual attention deficit disorder (SADD), because of my difficulty consistently focusing on my visions and dreams. For me, SADD manifests in many ways including, but not limited to: internal restlessness, distractions, boredom, racing thoughts, risk-taking, talking excessively, and agitation.

As far as I know, SADD is not a formal diagnosis but it is one I personally experience. There is no shame in seeking professional help for mental health or medical conditions. Over the years, I have participated in professional counseling to address depression and listlessness, which at times required prescribed psychotropic medication to manage my symptoms. Thank GOD for counselors and resources that helped me get back on track in my quest. Left untreated, depression has the power to sap my energy, cloud my thoughts and derail my visions and dreams. I declare war on everything and anything that attempts to neutralize my movement toward self-fulfillment. Let me emphasize: the only shame in having a mental disorder or medical condition is not seeking treatment from a qualified health professional. Remember, your visions and dreams are waiting for you. Seek the professional help you need. It is entirely possible to pursue your visions and dreams while taking care of your health.

CARE

I don't know about you, but at times I have acted as if I knew what was best for me. Here is another Sapphire story, and since this book is about truth telling, I accept and believe that GOD absolutely cares about my well-being and that GOD knows what is best for Melvina. One day in March 2021, I left home to go to the supermarket and stopped to have lunch at a Mexican restaurant. After ordering my food, the computerized cash register suddenly stopped working. The staff tried to fix it, but to no avail. Since the cash register couldn't be repaired at that moment, the staff gave me, and everyone in front of me, our lunches for free. Miraculously, the cash register started working right after we received our food. Okay GOD, thank you for showing me that You provide for my needs, that you are trustworthy, and that your promises never return to you void.

But wait, it gets better. That same day, I noticed Sweet Frog, a frozen yogurt establishment. It wasn't the first time I had seen it, but for some reason, that day it caught my attention. I sauntered in and I prepared my dessert. As I turned to sit down, I noticed a large sign on the wall near the door with the acronym FROG, Sweet Frog's mission statement. It stood for Fully Rely On GOD. Amazing! At that time, I was in the process of writing on the third Step, which reads: "We made a decision to turn our will and our lives over to the care of GOD as we understood Him."

It has often been said that there are no coincidences in life. My stop at Sweet Frog that day was clearly purposeful- to see the mission statement and to solidify the lesson that I must trust and rely on GOD no matter what.

A few days later, my husband and I visited a different Sweet Frog location, and then I went to yet another location, but the mission statement was not posted at either establishment. The moral of the experience? GOD often provides signs along the way to remind us that we can fully rely on and trust GOD's infinite wisdom and guidance. Many of you have likely experienced similar encounters and stories, too. GOD is always at work in our lives, if only we pay attention to the miracles, signs, and wonders before us. Isaiah 55:11 (NKJV) asserts: "So shall My word be that goes forth from My mouth; It shall not return to Me void, But it shall accomplish what I please, And it shall prosper in the thing for which I sent it."

CONFESSION

Spirituality offers us so many wonderful gifts, and confession is one of them. Today, let us accept the gift of confession as the powerful, spiritual gift that it is. In some faith traditions congregants have to confess to a priest, and if that is your tradition, follow what works for you. We also have the authority to confess our wrongdoings, misgivings and mistreatment of self and others directly to GOD in prayer.

The reason confession is mentioned here is because it is an essential ingredient and part of fulfilling our visions and dreams, at least I have found it to be necessary. What comes to mind when you read or hear the word confess? Traditionally, when some of us were asked to confess, it meant we had done something wrong. Perhaps our parents, grandparents, or some other authority figure sternly looked at you, shoulders squared with their feet firmly planted. If it were a woman, her hands would probably be on her hips. Couple that with their piercing eyes that seem to demand the truth about what happened in a particular situation or insist that you take responsibility for the broken or missing thingamajig. Whether guilty or not, we often experience a whirlwind of emotions: anger, guilt, shame, remorse, resentment, worthlessness, self-doubt, and the list goes on. Those are very powerful feelings. The fifth step of Narcotics Anonymous states it like this: "We admitted to GOD, to ourselves, and another human being the exact nature of our wrongs." James 5:16 (NIV) says it this way: "Therefore confess your sins to each other and pray for each other so that you may be healed. The prayer of a righteous person is powerful and effective."

Admittance and/or confession opens the door to FREEDOM from guilt and shame. Freedom ain't free, and neither is salvation. We have to relinquish some old ways of thinking and begin to get free of past and present issues that plague our spirits and inhibit us from moving toward our heart's desires.

CUISINE

Food. Most of us love delicious meals, I know I do. We need food for nourishment and fuel. On this journey, don't forget to eat. Some of us eat on the go or eat while driving. I don't know about you, but I rarely enjoy food when I'm driving or in transit, except when I'm eating and walking at a theme park, or a fair, etc. Food is meant to be enjoyed and savored. Over the past several years, I have been packing on pounds, and truthfully, I am not happy about it, but as we age and mature, weight gain is bound to happen. Unfortunately, during the coronavirus pandemic, most of us spent a great deal of time indoors with limited movement and interactions with others. The refrigerator was accessible 24/7. Before the Coronavirus pandemic, I spent 8–12 hours away from home, which made it a lot easier to manage my food intake. Over the past ten or so years, I have repeatedly embarked on a health and wellness journey as a part of my recovery process. The Living Clean: The Journey Continues states: "Sometimes praying for willingness can begin the process of change. An act as simple as preparing a proper meal for ourselves can be the first link in a new chain; as we incorporate healthy patterns in our lives, we begin to feel refreshed, renewed, and willing to set new goals for ourselves" (p. 99).

That makes so much sense to me. Recovery is far more than abstaining from illicit drugs and alcohol, it is a holistic journey that encompasses every aspect of my life. Being restored to a sense of well-being includes what I eat, as well. Caring for our physical selves is just as important as caring for our outer appearance. I tend to put a lot of effort into how I look to the outside world. Sometimes I neglect my inner life which consists of my thoughts, my attitudes, and my emotions.

You may have heard of mindfulness activities to calm yourself. Engaging in mindfulness allows us to be fully present and aware of where we are and what we are doing in the moment. There is also a benefit to employing mindfulness in my eating routine. As a member of a 12-Step fellowship, I recognize the importance of support no matter what my goals are. Left to my own devices, I can still self-destruct. To assist me on my health and wellness journey, I sought professional help. I also found a support group where others faced challenges with weight management. It was encouraging to hear women and men share their lifelong journeys with eating habits. It felt good to have people who identified with my struggles, and I gained so much insight and strength from them. In addition to support, I use an app that helps me record what and how much I eat, track my exercise routines, and much more. Suffice it to say, just for today, I am satisfied with my progress.

Disclaimer: We all have different dietary needs. Please consult your healthcare professional regarding your personal physical health requirements.

CARDIAC

Some years ago, I was prescribed medication for high blood pressure. In 2019, I was diagnosed with high cholesterol, which is a recipe for a heart condition. In 2020, I experienced a 95% blockage in my heart, which resulted in a stent being placed. The truth, what we've been exploring throughout this writing journey, is that I've had a heart condition long before that. My heart was broken at age 17 by my daughter's father, whom I loved, and who loved me too. As a seasoned woman now, I understand that we were both young, and his intentions were good. My heartbreak came because another girl was pregnant by him at the same time I was. My heart was crushed. At that time, I made a vow that no one would ever hurt me again, and I lived that out for a very, very, very, very, very, very, very long time, until now! That vow became deeply rooted in my psyche, so much so that I had forgotten that it was there. No wonder I tend to shut down emotionally and become distant.

I would be remiss not to mention my brother, who walked with me through that painful season. He was my anchor when I felt undone. Always supportive, always steady, he played an important role in my life, and in raising my daughter. Truth be told, he was more than an uncle to her— he was like a father. And for that I am profoundly grateful. My brother also stood by me during my early recovery journey. He gave me both accountability and safety when I needed them most.

But today, I declare and decree: I have reclaimed my heart. I am no longer a hostage to the past, and I no longer live on fantasy island. By practicing mindfulness, I remind myself that the original heartbreak occurred in 1976, and it belongs to that time period, not this present moment. That brings to my mind a book titled *The Body Keeps the Score: Brain, Mind, and Body in the Healing of Trauma.* I have not read the book in its entirety, but the title alone helped me understand how trauma impacts the whole self. I realized that as a teenager, I was traumatized by being in a love triangle that lasted until around 1979. I didn't have the skills or mindset to navigate that experience. In 1978, Gloria Gaynor's song *I Will Survive* came across the radio waves. She bellowed the lyrics, giving me the courage to end that chapter of my relationship. I Will Survive became my mantra for years. Tear-stained face, broken heart and all, I survived. I had some internal bleeding, but due to the recovery process,

I survived because I did the necessary work to identify, address and overcome heartbreak.

Disclaimer: I am not promoting or providing advice regarding heart issues. This is solely my personal experience and opinion about my own heart health.

CURRENCY (Money)

Financial health and wellness are essential to fulfilling your visions and dreams. Managing our finances and taking care of our responsibilities is simply the responsible thing to do. Many of us don't like the B word, just as we sometimes resist the F word, forgiveness. Do you know what the B word is? It's budgeting. Using a budget allows us to account for our spending habits. If you don't like the word budget, you can call it being fiscally responsible. There have been times when I was a stickler for a budget, but I have often strayed away from it. However, I am realizing now that mindful spending and saving are important, especially as I age. I want to live to be at least 100 years old, and I want to have the finances to take care of myself and enjoy the things I love.

Paying my bills on time is non-negotiable. Before going on vacation or enjoying time with friends, I make sure my financial obligations are taken care of first. I know people who go to conventions, concerts, travel abroad, shop, and eat out using money meant for their bills. After living it up, when their bills come due, they call friends for financial help. Don't be that person.

I grew up in the heart of Bushwick (Palmetto Street), Bedford-Stuyvesant (Bed-Stuy), and Brownsville, which was known as Burnsville in the 1960s and 1970s. We resided in raggedy tenements (abandominiums). The tenants often went without heat and hot water for months at a time. As I write this, I am keenly aware that my mother and the other families did the best they could with meager resources.

My nuclear family was raised on welfare. Sometimes there wasn't enough food to feed our family of seven or eight, but my mother made do with what she had. Neighbors helped each other with a borrowed cup of sugar, rice, flour, butter, or detergent. In a real sense, they were a community of believers because they supported each other during difficult, trying, and joyous times. I share this because I know what it means to live in poverty, to be hungry, to face homelessness, and to be cold. Despite these challenges, my mother ensured our clothing was clean and that her children ate first. Our kitchen cabinets and refrigerator were filled with welfare cheese, canned meat, yellow grits, and whatever else the government provided to families like ours.

I have evolved from rags to riches, and today I am by far wealthier than my mother ever was. While I appreciate having monetary resources to meet my basic needs and some of my wants, I am declaring war on being irresponsible with my discretionary funds. I have student loan debt and credit card debt, which need to be addressed promptly. My goal is to meet with a financial planner. A friend once told me, if you don't give money a purpose, it will evaporate like mist. That makes so much sense, and I've been putting that strategy into practice ever since.

For some of us, including me, being fiscally responsible can be challenging because of our insatiable appetite for clothes, boots, shoes, jewelry, perfume, pocketbooks, hats, suits, and so on. But don't be dismayed; you can declare war on unhealthy spending habits, too. As I continue to matriculate through life, I will be in a better financial position, and have the currency and resources to fund my visions and dreams. Let's do this together!

CHAMPION

Go, you champion. YOU, yes YOU, and me too. I am a champion and you are a champion because we have overcome many challenges, and I still have more fight in me, and so do you. There are visions and dreams I have yet to fulfill. Since the 1990's I have listened to various motivational speakers. One of my favorites is Les Brown who says you have to be hungry to win at life, and I certainly agree.

Over the past few months, I've started listening to athletes who are champions in their sport. I realized that champions have a distinct mindset about winning. Basketball, football, and baseball are team-driven sports, so to win, you have to rely on the team and the coach. Yet it's equally important to understand your role and what you bring to the experience. Many of these athletes, men and women alike share one thing in common: they decided to be the best of the best, even if they weren't at the top of their game at the time. Surprisingly, many of them spoke about feeling insecure or inadequate, but they did not allow those unproductive thoughts (chit-chat) to deter them from their goals. Champions train not only their bodies, but also their minds to win. Proverbs 22:6 says it this way: "Train up a child (mind) in the way she/he should go, and when she/he is old, she/he will not depart from you."

The same is true of the mind; I have to train my mind in the direction I want it to go because, left unattended, my mind and the unproductive "chit-chat" can lead me astray. If we're not careful, that inner chatter can sneak into our thoughts and thwart GOD's plans. By now, you know the voice I am referring to, because we've been discussing it throughout these pages.

Two of my favorite sports are basketball and boxing. My favorite basketball team has always been the Los Angeles Lakers, particularly the 1980's dream team (sorry New York Knicks fans). I used to watch basketball and boxing constantly, though not as much these days.

A few months ago, I came across a YouTube video of Mike Tyson, and I immediately admired him for several reasons. Mike Tyson and I are from the same hood, Brownsville, one of the most impoverished communities back in the 1960s, later revitalized in the 1990s. I wasn't particularly drawn to Tyson's physical fighting techniques, but his dogged mentality fascinated me. I call it dogged because he fought with a no matter what attitude. He aimed to win by any means necessary, even if it meant biting his opponent's ear. LOL! Dang, Mike went in for the kill because he was hungry to win. His boxing license was revoked after that incident, but later reinstated. Growing up in poverty creates a hunger that is hard to explain. Champions are champions because they have an insatiable drive to succeed, no matter what. Just in case you're wondering, fellow Sojourner, I will not be biting anyone, but as a native New Yorker, I am taking a bite out of the Big Apple.

There have been countless people who inspired me on my journey, and one of them is Susan Taylor, the former editor and chief of *Essence Magazine*. I especially loved reading her column, *In The Spirit* where she encouraged readers to embrace their uniqueness and to live their dreams out loud. In 1998, while serving as president of the Student Government Association at my alma mater, Audrey Cohen College, (now Metropolitan College of New York), I had the privilege and pleasure of escorting Ms. Taylor to a college-sponsored event where she was the keynote speaker. For so many years, I admired her from afar; never did I dream I would meet her in the flesh. I was nervous and exhilarated at once. What do you say and how do you behave, in the presence of such a spiritual giant? In that moment, I chose to simply be myself; I was 40 years old then, and it's hard to believe that was more than 25 years ago. Ms. Taylor inquired about my future goals, and I shared that I planned to attend seminary after graduation. She was just as nurturing and caring in person as she was on the pages of Essence. She listened with that signature twinkle in her eyes, a reflection of both her inward and outward beauty. Being in Ms. Taylor's presence was an unforgettable experience, one I reflect on from time to time to remember both where I came from and where I am headed.

CEREMONY

This is the culmination of the journey within. It may be beyond your wildest imagination, but let's be open-minded together. Where are you at friend; are you still here? You didn't give up right before the miracle, did you?

There is one last thing I want to invite you to do as we conclude this journey. Get ready because this one might be a shocker. Most of us think about getting married, but have you ever thought about marrying YOU? It is a novel and innovative idea, isn't it? Imagine pledging your undying love, faith, and dedication to GOD's vision, purposes, and plans for your life. Envision the contentment and joy you will experience when you make yourself important to you. Marrying oneself is not to the exclusion of marrying someone else, or divorcing or leaving your partner if you are currently in a committed relationship. I believe that when women in particular and people in general give themselves what we so readily and freely give to others, our lives will improve significantly. Self-love is the law of preservation. We attract to ourselves who and what we are, so get busy loving yourself. It is important to love the self you are right now. Never mind focusing on your flaws and defects. There is more to you than meets the physical eye. You are made in the image and likeness of GOD (Gen. 1:27). So, go forth, recognizing that you can do anything you put your mind to.

Plan a commitment ceremony like no other event you've ever planned and organized. This one's for you, my friend and fellow sojourner. Make it what you want it to be. The commitment ceremony is not about extravagance, although if you want to go all out, then by all means do what makes your heart content. For those who can't afford to or have no desire to plan an extravaganza, create and design a commitment celebration that reflects your authentic self, based on your resources and values. Remember, there is no pressure to compete with anyone else. You can invite friends, or you can do it privately. It's really up to you.

Some ideas for creating a ceremony are: baptism or re-baptism, rededication, plan a small gathering comprised of your community of believers to celebrate with you, have a pool/beach party, go to a museum, participate in a community effort, join or start a book club are some considerations. Be creative and honor your journey.

Whatever and however you choose to celebrate your commitment, take that leap of FAITH. In the words of Iyanla

Vanzant, I say to you, "Make your life an act of faith." On her CD titled *Expressions of My Mind*, Tulani Kinard recorded a song titled "Make Your Life an Act of Faith." That album is my go-to when I need to remember who I am. There are so many inspiring songs on the soundtrack.

Please, my fellow sojourner, always remember that your journey might twist and turn (remember the labyrinth). Anticipate that there will be days when you don't want to participate in your own life, and that it is okay. When you are ready to resume the journey, just continue from where you left off. No judgment, and no self-criticism from me, and hopefully you will be gentle with yourself. Employ your spiritual practices of affirmative prayer & meditation, and/or do one of the clearing, cleansing, or clowning activities to jump-start your life. Please, just be gentle and kind with yourself, NO MATTER WHAT!

CELEBRATION

On this journey I started out as a caterpillar, and at last I have emerged as a beautiful colorful butterfly. Wow, transformation feels amazing, but it did not come without a cost. Yet, the view from up here is magnificent, and now it is time to soar. Are you ready to celebrate? Some of you may remember the 1981 song by Skyy: *Let's Celebrate!* Back in the day we used to cut a rug when that song came on! Well, I am celebrating right now because I have finally finished writing this book. I'm dancing all across my house with joy and gratitude. The bible says: "Finally, brothers and sisters, whatsoever things are true, whatsoever things are noble, whatsoever things are right, whatsoever things are pure, whatsoever things are lovely, whatsoever things are admirable, if anything is excellent or praiseworthy—think about such things. Whatsoever you have learned or received or heard from me, or seen in me—put it into practice (for your enrichment). And the GOD of peace will be with you" (Phil 4:8-9, NIV).

And that my fellow sojourners, concludes The Caterpillar Chronicles: Awakening and Becoming in the Dance of Recovery. Go forth, live your life out loud, and never be afraid to spread your wings.

REFERENCES

Arterburn, S, & Stoop, D. (1998). *The Life Recovery Bible NLT*. Tyndale House Publishers.

Narcotics Anonymous World Services. *Living Clean: The Journey Continues*. (2012). Van Nuys, CA. Narcotics Anonymous World Services.

Narcotics Anonymous World Services. (2008). Narcotic Anonymous (6th ed.) Van Nuys, CA.

Paulus, T. (1972). *Hope for the Flowers*. New Jersey: Paulus Press.

Pressfield, S. (2002). *The War of Art: Break Through the Blocks and Win Your Inner Creative Battles*. New York: Rugged Land.

Van der Kolk, Bessel. (2014). *The Body Keeps the Score: Brain, Mind, and Body in the Healing of Trauma*. New York. Penguin Books.

The Caterpillar Chronicles:

Awakening and Becoming in the Dance of Recovery

Melvina Y. Goodman

This is a story of transformation, faith, and growth. Melvina shares how she moved through hidden seasons of challenge, much like a caterpillar in its cocoon, and emerged like a butterfly—renewed, strengthened, and ready to soar.

Spiritually, she experienced an awakening, cultivating a more authentic connection with God. Professionally, she embraced her calling as a preacher, counselor, educator, and leader, while also nurturing growth and love in her family life and friendships.

Within this book, you'll find enriching activities to support your own journey of becoming and your dance of recovery. The Caterpillar Chronicles shows that becoming is a lifelong journey—and now, Melvina invites you to embark on or continue your own spiritual path of awakening. Are you ready to come out of the cocoon and emerge into a beautiful butterfly? Fantabulous—let's soar!

About the Author

Melvina Y. Goodman is a pastor, professor, and counselor with over 35 years of experience in addiction recovery, education, and spiritual care. A proud Brooklyn native, she has dedicated her life to helping individuals overcome adversity and embrace transformation. Melvina holds a Bachelor's degree in Human Services from Metropolitan College of New York, a Master of Divinity from Virginia Union University, and two Master of Science degrees from Virginia Commonwealth University—one in Patient Counseling (Chaplaincy) and the other in Rehabilitation Counseling. She is a Licensed Professional Counselor (LPC), Certified Substance Abuse Counselor (CSAC), Certified Rehabilitation Counselor (CRC), Master Addictions Counselor (MAC), and Certified Life Coach.

Melvina teaches group dynamics and substance abuse counseling courses at Reynolds Community College in Richmond, Virginia, where she is known for her dynamic teaching, authenticity, and compassion. Her journey from adversity to purpose fuels her mission to inspire others to reclaim their lives, walk in faith, and live fully.

Personal Statement: Truly, my GOD has traveled with me on this fantastic voyage called life. As I reflect on my life, I am in awe of how GOD has orchestrated my life and weaved it into such a beautiful tapestry. My intention is to be all that GOD has designed me to be, to reach excellence in all that I do, and to help others reach their fullest potential.